THE LANGUAGE AND USES OF RIGHTS

A Biopsy of American Jurisprudence in the Twentieth Century

Samuel J. M. Donnelly

UNIVERSITY PRESS OF AMERICA

Lanham • New York • London

University Press of America®, Inc.
4720 Boston Way
Lanham, Maryland 20706

3 Henrietta Street
London WC2E 8LU England

Printed in the United States of America
British Cataloging in Publication Information Available

Library of Congress Cataloging-in-Publication Data

Donnelly, Samuel J.M.
The language and uses of rights : a biopsy of American jurisprudence in the twentieth century / Samuel J.M. Donnelly.
p. cm.
Includes bibliographical references and index.
1. Law – United States – Philosophy. 2. Jurisprudence – United States. 3. Natural law. 4. Law – Language. I. Title.
KF379.D66 349.73—dc20 [347.3] 93–40757 CIP

ISBN 0–8191–9405–0 (pbk. : alk. paper)

™ The paper used in this publication meets the minimum requirements of American National Standard for Information Sciences—Permanence of Paper for Printed Library Materials, ANSI Z39.48–1984.

For My Students

Contents

Preface

Once upon a time, it was customary to offer definitions of law. Oliver Wendell Holmes, Jr., described law as the predictions of what courts would, in fact, do. He wisely added his comment that the life of the law has not been logic but experience. John Austin defined law as the command of the sovereign backed by sanctions. After refuting Austin in the early chapters of *The Concept of Law*, H. L. A. Hart offered his own elucidation of law as a system composed of primary rules of obligation and secondary rules of recognition, change and adjudication which tell us how to use primary rules. Hart's vision of law, then, was as a system of rules. While insisting on the role of the judge, American Pragmatists such as Roscoe Pound and Karl Llewellyn refrained from offering any definition of law, they preferred to emphasize what went into rather than what was not part of law.

Rather than a definition, this book offers a vision of law as an activity engaged in by a variety of players including judges, advocates for the plaintiff and defendant, law reformers, scholars and perhaps all of us. The use of language, particularly the language of rights, is an important aspect of that activity. Rights discourse, the use of the language of rights by those engaged in the activity of law, is employed as contended subsequently to establish, talk about, fight about, and change relations between persons. The description and analysis of rights discourse offered in this book is an illustration of the vision of law as an activity.

During the twentieth century a variety of scholars have offered definitions or analysis of rights. Some have looked upon rights discourse skeptically or have found it politically inconvenient. In contrast, H. L. A. Hart viewed rights discourse in his inaugural lecture, "Definition and Theory in Jurisprudence," as language usage. Following that hint, this book analyzes various understandings of rights offered during the century as language usages, ways of using the language of rights. That analysis is initially set forth in Chapter I, the Introduction, and at greater length in Chapter II. Later after further foundation it is contended that the great use of rights discourse is to conduct a conversation between persons in different horizons in a pluralist society. By recording and analyzing various understandings of rights offered by scholars in the twentieth century Chapters I and II present a slice of the century's jurisprudential life which some may find useful as an overview, a review or an introduction.

Chapter III introduces and elucidates the notion of Horizons and thereby plunges into the middle of current discussion which perceives all statements including statements regarding rights as made within cultural contexts, that is within Horizons. After and in view of the discussion of Horizons a Model for understanding rights discourse is offered and applied to the various understandings of rights described in Chapters I and II.

In *The Concept of Law*, H. L. A. Hart provides an understanding of obligation and the acceptance of law perceived from the internal perspective of those who use rules to justify conduct. Chapter IV offers a higher interpretation of rights discourse from that perspective which enables us to perceive conversation across the multiple horizons in a pluralist society as an important use of the language of rights. Rights language is used to appeal to obligations of others as perceived within their horizons.

An important human commitment shared by many is to afford all persons deep respect and concern. The obligations which flow from that commitment would support a non-skeptical understanding of rights. One obligation would be to engage in conversation with persons in foreign horizons in an effort to understand and respect their assertions of rights. Many persons who use rights discourse internally accept rights and relate their statements concerning rights to obligations they perceive themselves as having. H. L. A. Hart's internal point of view, then, offers an opportunity to relate the language of rights to persons and their internal self-understanding. From that perspective, the language and uses of rights are means for relating persons to each other despite their multiple different horizons.

The slice of twentieth century jurisprudential life offered in this book and the vision of rights discourse as an aspect of law seen as an activity relating persons to each other is part of a larger project--to understand law in relation to persons. This book presents then only a part of a larger vision and should be perceived as offering a set of narrow insights rather than being an attempt to define law or to paint the grand picture. Here through analysis and description, rights discourse, an aspect of the activity of law, is understood as a means for relating persons in our pluralist society, a society composed of multiple horizons.

Acknowledgments

The author wants to thank his research assistants, Kurt Summers, Elizabeth Little, Dan Falge and Sandeep Qusba for their invaluable assistance in the preparation of footnotes and other research. I also want to thank Clare Doerle, Margaret Smith, and Mary Ann McClanahan, secretaries at the Syracuse University College of Law and Edward Graham, computer consultant at the College of Law for their help in preparing the manuscript.

Acknowledgments

[illegible]

Chapter I

Purposes and Basic Insights

If human relations are at the core of the game of life, then rights are important tools in that game, significant means by which persons establish, change, talk about, fight about, reconcile, and struggle with human relations. The purpose of this book is to clarify the discussion of rights and to contribute to our understanding of their relevance to the on-going process of creating, changing and conversing about relations between persons.

One could describe the history of Anglo-American legal philosophy in the twentieth century as a grand conversation.[1] Rights and the effort to understand their meaning and function have been major themes of that conversation. H.L.A. Hart, who has engaged in discussions with many leading legal philosophers, including the legal realists, Lon Fuller, and Ronald Dworkin, could be described as the host of the salon, the catalyst for the grand conversation.[2] The Crits, members of the movement described as Critical Legal Studies, could be perceived as party crashers who have significant insights regarding rights and human relations but who want to change the terms of the conversation.[3]

In fact, as the gate-crashers have multiplied and the Critical Legal Studies Movement has begun to dissolve into

Feminist Jurisprudence,[4] Outsider Jurisprudence[5] and other allied movements many influenced by Post-Modernism, the opportunity for and possibility for conversation may appear to vanish. That impression, I believe, is misleading. James Boyd White offers an understanding of law as rhetoric which is capable of reestablishing the Grand Conversation and of offering an understanding of the game of law itself as a conversation about what our society and legal institutions shall be.[6] Recently new partners in conversation have appeared. Judge Posner is diligently learning from and absorbing the insights of Robin West who herself is engaged diligently in relating visions of law to each other.[7]

A second purpose of this book is to offer a slice of the history of legal philosophy and an insight into that grand conversation by abstracting from it various differing understandings of the uses of rights and the language of rights.[8] As one reviews the discussions of rights, it is possible to catalog some uses of rights or of the language of rights. That catalog would include the following:

1. Rights as Conclusions: If we view law as a system of rules, then the assertion that X has a right is a way of drawing a conclusion within that legal system. H. L. A. Hart offered the analysis of rights as conclusions within a system of rules for the purpose of correcting the legal realist claim that there is no right in the absence of a remedy.[9]

2. Rights as Remedies: A person has a legal right when one can make a prediction that courts will recognize that right and afford a remedy. The legal realists asserted that this is the only meaningful way to describe a legal right.[10]

3. Rights as Trumps: When a government such as that of the United States is subject to a constitution which protects minority rights, then a successful assertion of rights will

trump decisions of the government or the majority, just as in bridge a two of trumps will defeat the ace of a non-trump suit.[11]

4. Rights as Reasons: When a judge declares a state action or statute unconstitutional he may assert that it violates a provision of the constitution such as the due process clause of the 14th Amendment [12] or the prohibition of cruel and unusual punishment in the 8th Amendment.[13] The statute, then, is declared unconstitutional, because it violates a party's right to due process or not to be subjected to cruel and unusual punishment.[14] The party's right, then, is the reason for declaring the state action or statute unconstitutional.

When a constitutional provision such as one of those mentioned in the last paragraph is open-textured, then a judge may refer to a background theory of justice or rights as a basis for interpreting the open-textured language and choosing between alternate results. For example, a background theory concerning a right to human dignity may be the reason a judge offers for an interpretation of the prohibition of cruel and unusual punishment. The right to human dignity, then, is the reason for the interpretation of the right not to be subjected to cruel and unusual punishment and both are reasons for declaring the state action or statute unconstitutional.[15]

Ultimately the judge's understanding of the law, of rights, or of the Constitution may be grounded in a yet more comprehensive theory or interpretation. The judge may argue that his fundamental theory or interpretation not only has good institutional fit but that it offers a higher understanding of or makes the most that one can out of the law or the Constitution.[16]

5. Rights as Goals: A right to economic development set forth in an international document[17] or claimed by a group

or an underdeveloped country is not a trump in the sense that the right to free speech can trump a government policy of promoting a war effort. The right cannot be immediately enforced by a court. Rather it is a goal to be pursued over time by appropriate measures. If there is a right to economic development it is a right to pursue a goal or to have assistance in pursuing a goal.

Those who perceive law or judicial decisions as based on policies may understand rights in general as goals to be pursued.[18] For example, equality or more specifically racial equality can be understood as an important national goal or policy to be achieved by appropriate and effective means such as school integration or bussing.[19] Rights such as freedom of the press may be understood as instrumental rights designed to serve the goal of promoting robust discussion in a democratic society.[20] State libel laws can be modified because they interfere with that constitutional right, that is, they interfere with the goal of promoting robust discussion.[21] In this last example, rights understood as goals are compatible with rights as trumps.

6. <u>Rights as Claims</u>: When a litigant first asserts a right before it has been recognized by a court, it is a claim.[22] Likewise someone may assert before a legislature an as yet unrecognized right as the basis for legislation. That assertion would also be a claim.

7. <u>Rights as Criticism:</u> The writer of a law review article may disagree with a judicial decision and may assert a right either recognized or unrecognized as the foundation for the disagreement. In this usage, the assertion of a right is a criticism.[23]

8. <u>Rights as Resources</u>: When engaged in political action the members of an interest group may assert rights either recognized or unrecognized in the course of speeches, in advertisements, in litigation, or before legislatures. One

reason for these assertions and the activity surrounding them may be to promote the rights asserted. However, there may be other reasons for the assertions such as to rally one's supporters, provide them with a slogan or to weaken and repel one's opponents. The ultimate purpose may be to advance the group's varied interests and not merely to maintain the rights asserted. The assertions of rights are resources for promoting other group interests.[24]

9. Crits (Rights as Ideology?): Various members of the movement known as Critical Legal Studies have expressed outrage at, distaste for, or disagreement with rights discourse in Anglo-American law or legal philosophy.[25] Among their critical comments are the following. Rights as understood in the dominant discourse are excessively abstract and not related to people, situations, or experience. As a result, there is a pretense of objectivity in rights discourse. Indeed, as H.L.A. Hart once asserted, rights drawn as conclusions within a system of rules may be morally wrong[26] and may represent the interests of the economically dominant and oppressing class. An example would be the historical property right of a master to own a slave which was a conclusion drawn in the American legal system during the early nineteenth century. Those working with law rather than focusing on rights rhetoric should be concerned with who is oppressed in a situation. Rather than concern for rights within a community, there should be an emphasis upon responsibility, interconnectedness, and the manner in which each person in the community is part of and related to the others. Rights as understood in the dominant discourse are excessively individualistic, are related to isolated individuals and may tend to isolate them. Ultimately, rights as presently understood are grounded in the liberal imagination born during the Enlightenment with its abstract and excessively individualistic concept of the

human person.[27]

Despite their problems with rights, Crits, for reasons of tactics, strategy, or criticism engage, or would engage, in many of the forms of rights discourse described above. To advance the movement or a particular ideological cause Crits would use rights as claims, criticism and perhaps most often as resources. While the Crits like H.L.A. Hart view rights as part of an inherited system of rules, they use rights as means for change and struggle, as tools in the game of life, as they perceive that game.[28]

For example, see Duncan Kennedy's use of first amendment freedom of speech rights in his article, "Freedom and Constraint in Adjudication: A Critical Phenomenology".[29] After his imaginary judge recharacterizes the request for a labor injunction as an attempt at prior restraint of freedom of speech, he uses that right to advance his ideological goal of affording workers greater control over the means of production.[30] See likewise Roberto Unger's discussion of destabilization rights in his essay, "The Critical Legal Studies Movement," where he also classifies rights in his imaginary society as (i) immunity rights, (ii) destabilization rights, (iii) market rights, (iv) solidarity rights.[31] That analysis of rights contains a number of significant insights but it also is the use of rights in the service of an ideologically supported redesign of society. The Crits attack current and past uses of rights as related to establishment ideology and the dominant group's social and economic interests.[32] Consistently, then, they propose to use rights in the service of their own ideological goals and to promote ideological ends in a redesigned society.

10. <u>Rights as Rhetoric</u>: James Boyd White in *Heracles' Bow* contends that law should be understood as rhetoric, that is, as an ongoing conversation or argument about what

our society and legal institutions shall be.[33] Many of the uses of rights set forth above could be misdescribed as rhetoric in the bad sense of clever tools of persuasion. White offers a better understanding of rhctoric as persuasion by the sharing of experience. Rights discourse could be understood in that sense as a calling of attention to one's own experience, for example, of oppression, or an appeal to the other person's commitment or experience.

The modern use of narrative in law also is a calling of attention to one's own experience or an appeal to the common human experience of others. Robin West in a recent work has examined the use of narrative and rights discourse in Supreme Court opinions and has suggested the alternate use of each for similar purposes.[34]

A. Problems of Rights Discourse

There are at least two problems with the traditional understanding of rights:

1. In traditional legal discourse and in the popular imagination, rights are too narrowly perceived as conclusions drawn within a system of rules, whether that system be the prevailing legal system or some system of moral rules. Perhaps influenced by the liberal imagination we view rights individualistically as entitlements of individuals rather than as means of conducting human relations. Entitlements (or rights as entitlements) are perceived as valid because they are conclusions drawn within the legal system. The Crits as well as others tend to understand rights in this narrow fashion and hence perceive them as abstract, as part of the established legal system and as embodiments of the interests of the dominant and oppressing class which controls the legal system, the system of rules.

2. As the Crits perceive we understand rights within an inherited framework established by our political, social, and cultural as well as our legal background. This framework and hence our understanding of rights, including particular rights, may be influenced by our economic and other interests. In this book, horizons, a word derived from European philosophy,[35] will be used to describe the frameworks which establish and restrict our vision, our understanding of legal concepts, rules, and rights. Failure to account for horizons in our understanding of rights contributes to a misunderstanding in which rights are perceived abstractly, as conclusions within systems of rules, and removed from the give and take of human relations.

The grand conversation of legal philosophy in the twentieth century not only has discussed differing understandings of rights but has illustrated many differing uses of rights and the language of rights, for example, those listed in the catalog set forth above.[36] By setting forth a portion of that grand conversation one can trace the progress we have made in departing from a simplified model of rights, describe a series of uses of rights, and show the manner in which rights are understood and used within horizons, the horizons of the legal philosophies participating in the grand conversation. The next part of this book will undertake the task just described. (Chapter II).

The third part of the book (Chapter III) will discuss the problem of horizons and rights understood within horizons using illustrations from the grand conversation. Important to that discussion will be a simpler understanding of rights or the language of rights used from different points of view, for example, the point of view of plaintiff's counsel, defendant's counsel or the judge.[37] That discussion will account for the problem of horizons and will allow us to perceive the manner in which rights are used to carry forward human relations, that is to establish, change, talk about, fight about, reconcile and struggle with human relations.

A higher interpretation (Chapter IV)[38] of the role of rights is as a means of conducting a conversation concerning human relations between persons who have different horizons which allow them to perceive rights and relations differently. The grand conversation in Anglo-American legal philosophy during the twentieth century is an example of such a conversation. Where vital human interests are more immediately at stake than in the grand conversation, an important use of rights in conversation between persons with different horizons is to appeal to the other person's sense of obligation or fundamental commitment. Following discussion of that use of rights, it may be possible to restate the traditional understanding of rights as individual entitlements while accounting for the problem of horizons and perceiving rights not as conclusions drawn within a legal system but as means for human relations. That restatement would recognize that one person can speak meaningfully of his rights where he can hypothesize, demand, claim, or perceive that another person has an obligation,[39] an obligation which may arise from commitment to a legal system, a moral system, a fundamental moral principle, an ideological cause, or to respect for humanity or the fundamental humanity of each person. The restatement will recognize that rights and the language of rights are used within and across horizons to appeal to obligations which others recognize or which it is claimed they should recognize. Such appeals are made in the course of establishing, changing, talking about, fighting about, reconciling and struggling with human relations. For those enamored of more traditional philosophical precision, one can codify this restatement in a formula: X has a right where Y has an obligation. Either X or Y, or both, may be hypothetical, and may have differing roles such as the roles of plaintiff, defendant, parties to the contract, judge and party to a lawsuit, developed country and member of an undeveloped country, and so on. X and Y may share horizons or have different horizons. Chapter IV[40] of the book will conclude with this restatement of the meaning of rights. It is a restatement which perceives rights as essentially relational and as part of the human struggle, the game of life.

Chapter II

The Grand Conversation of Legal Philosophy In the Twentieth Century

A. Introduction

Over the course of the twentieth century since the early legal realist attack on formalism,[41] we have developed a much more sophisticated understanding of laws. The purpose of this chapter is to trace the progress we have made in departing from the excessively simplified model of rights presented by formalism. The danger which is difficult to avoid is the development of a new model itself excessively simplified to replace the one rejected. A corresponding danger is that recognizing the inadequacy of all our models we will reject all. The Crits impatient with abstractions may encounter that danger; a rejection of rights discourse itself may be an oversimplification.

In the introduction a catalog of various uses of rights was presented.[42] By elaborating that catalog and discussing the philosophical understandings supporting each view of the function of rights, a foundation will be laid for developing a more sophisticated model of rights capable of accounting for each use of rights. During the discussion of the various uses of rights it will be possible to recognize and illustrate the manner in which we perceive rights within horizons and from a point of view, a topic which will be presented at greater length in the next part of the book (Chapter III).[43]

The discussion, then, should begin with the attack on formalism and H. L. A. Hart's comments on that attack.

B. Hart and the Realists: Rights as Remedies v. Rights as Conclusions in a System of Rules

H. L. A. Hart may be understood better if one perceives significant aspects of his thought as part of a conversation with the legal realists.[44] This is particularly true of his understanding of rights as described in his inaugural address, "Definition and Theory in Jurisprudence."[45]

In turn legal realism arose in a historical context, the context of an attack on legal formalism and a campaign for social reform, and can be better understood after reviewing that context.[46] H. L. A. Hart defines formalism as follows:

> the vice known to legal theory as formalism or conceptualism consists in an attitude to verbally formulated rules which both seeks to disguise and to minimize the need for ... choice, once the general rule has been laid down.47

In the latter nineteenth and early twentieth centuries a Supreme Court heavily influenced by formalism declared unconstitutional a number of social reforms enacted by Congress and the state legislatures.[48] One response of the reformers, particularly but not exclusively that portion of the reformers known as legal realists was to attack the intellectual foundations of formalism.[49] Llewellyn, for example, insisted that the law was full of leeways created in part by the many different orthodox ways of dealing with precedent.[50] That position, controversial in its time, now has the flavor of ordinary and routine knowledge about law. A more radical and still controversial attack on the roots of formalism was rule skepticism. Llewellyn emphasized the difference between paper rules found in statutes, the holdings of cases, and treatises and the real rules actually applied by judges in the decision of cases.[51] He accepted Holmes definition - "[t]he prophecies of what the courts will do in fact, and nothing more pretentious are what I mean by the law".[52] He argued, then, that the paper rules were not a basis for predicting the actual decisions of judges.[53] He urged empirical research as a way of predicting judges decisions and hence of discovering the real rules.[54] However, his rule skepticism also can be perceived as an attack on the certainty and usefulness of the paper rules which dominated legal formalism. By weakening adherence to paper rules legal realists would clarify the need for policy choices and proper policy decision making which would advance the cause of social reform.[55]

H. L. A. Hart accepted the need for flexibility, choice, and policy decision making in the development and application of legal rules.[56] However, he rejected rule skepticism.[57] In *The Concept of Law* he characterizes "Formalism and rule-sceptism" as the "Scylla and Charybdis of juristic theory."[58] He explains that formalism and rule skepticism "are great exaggerations, salutary where they correct each other" and claimed that "the truth lies between them."[59] Hart accepts some of the insights of rule skepticism and agrees fully with Llewellyn's claim that the law is full of leeways.[60] In *The Concept of Law* he offers a clarifying concept, the open-texture of law, which reconciles his basic rejection of rule skepticism with acceptance of such legal realist insights as leeways in law, the importance of flexibility, choice and policy decision making, and the difficulty of predicting judicial decisions. He explains open-texture as follows:

> Whichever device, precedent or legislation, is chosen for the communication of standards of behavior...will, at some point where their application is in question, prove indeterminate; they will have what has been termed an *open-texture*. So far we have presented this, in the case of legislation, as a general feature of human language; uncertainty at the borderline is the price to be paid for the use of general classifying terms in any form of communication concerning matters of fact. Natural languages like English are when so used irreducibly *open-textured*. It is, however, important to appreciate why, apart from this dependence on language as it actually is, with its characteristics of open-texture, we should not cherish, even as an ideal, the conception of a rule so detailed that the question whether it applied or not to a particular case was always settled in advance, and never involved, at the point of actual application, a fresh choice between open alternatives. Put shortly, the reason is that the necessity for such choice is thrust upon us because we are men, not gods.[61]

Open textured concepts and rules have a clear core meaning which applies to generally accepted instances. However, there is a shadowy or penumbral area where the concept or rule may or may not apply.[62] Judges, then, who may be imagined as deputy legislators have the task of choosing in penumbral area cases whether or not to apply the concept or rule and may make their decisions on the basis of sound policy criteria. In penumbral cases there is flexibility and the necessity for choice but there remains an important role for paper rules. They are the basic means of communicating standards of behavior and will prevail in clear core instances.[63] Hart has accepted Llewellyn's leeways but largely has rejected his rule skepticism.

Llewellyn's insistence that one has a right only when it is predictable that the court will afford a remedy is grounded in Holmes' predictive theory of law and in Llewellyn's rule skepticism. Paper rules protecting rights are nevertheless paper rules and high theories, moral or political, which support rights are even less reliable as a basis for predicting the decisions of courts.[64] Real rights as opposed to paper rights exist when the courts will afford a remedy.[65] This harsh view of rights can be understood better in the context of the drive for social reform. One should not speak vaguely or in high moral terms about rights, but one should determine what rights the courts are actually enforcing. Then one should campaign vigorously for enforcement of additional rights. Llewellyn explained this position most clearly in one of the songs he used to decorate his books: "Some say our law is headed for perdition. The answer to that is to set it right in the Common Law Tradition."[66]

Hart concerned ever with language and hence with paper rules rejected rights skepticism as he rejected rule skepticism. His analysis of rights skepticism in his speech, "Definition and Theory in Jurisprudence",[67] nevertheless reflects respect for the realist insight. He is concerned likewise with the language philosopher's distaste for meaningless language,[68] that is, language that has no hard reference point. Llewellyn may have a similar concern.[69] A statement that X has a right has a hard reference point that can be empirically verified when it is equated with a prediction that the courts will afford a remedy.

As a language philosopher Hart wants to examine how language is used. In the way we use language concerning rights he finds the hard reference point that makes that language meaningful and at the same time affords a role for the paper rules. The assertion, X has a right to be paid ten pounds by Y, assumes the existence of a legal system or a system of rules, "the operation of the sanctions of the system, and the general likelihood that this will continue."[70] "A statement of the form 'X has a right' is used [then] to draw a conclusion of law in a particular case which falls under such rules."[71] That conclusion may be drawn by a judge or other official. In "Definition and Theory in Jurisprudence" Hart offers the example of a referee in a game of cricket who declares a player out.[72] The referee is an official drawing a conclusion within the system of rules which constitute the game of cricket. However, despite the finality of the referee's decision, a fan's contrary statement that the player is safe, is a meaningful statement. The fan also draws a conclusion within the system of rules which constitutes the game of cricket. While the referee has made a final ruling the fan's statement can be understood as criticism, an assertion that in the circumstances the referee drew the wrong conclusions in the system of rules.[73] The hard reference point here is not the remedy but the system of rules. Others can refer to the system of rules to verify the fan's criticism. Likewise in law a Supreme Court decision may be final but subject to criticism by a law review article. The criticism in the article is meaningful because it refers to hard reference points, the system of rules that constitutes the law and the orthodox techniques for drawing conclusions within that system of rules. Hart would note, then, that a statement that X has a right is a conclusion drawn within a system of rules by an official, by a critic, or by one making a claim in the legal system.[74] Although those criticizing or making claims may not be predicting official rulings or remedies their statements are meaningful because they refer to the system of rules.

Hart respects the legal realist insistence upon a hard reference point for statements of rights and their interest in predicting official rulings but finds Llewellyn's definition of rights as predictions of remedies too narrow.[75] Llewellyn's definition misses a number of meaningful uses of language concerning rights. Making claims and criticizing official decisions are significant and useful actions within our legal system.

C. Rights as Trumps; Rights as Reasons

H. L. A. Hart's conversations and influence span much of the jurisprudence of the twentieth century. Ronald Dworkin is one of his latest partners in dialogue.[76] Dworkin's thought emerges in part from further progress on the battlefront of human rights.[77] The legal realists were part of the law reform effort to overcome formalism. Hart's conversation with the realists is part of the attempt to set the excesses and insights of the reform movement in order. However, the work of the Warren Court led a second great era of twentieth century law reform. The defeat of formalism, the insistence that law is open-textured, flexible and full of leeways and the policy oriented pragmatism of the legal realists and others had prepared the way for the Warren Court. Its work was challenged, however, precisely because it was policy oriented and pragmatic.[78] The critics of the Warren Court argued for a more principled approach to legal decision making.[79]

In *Taking Rights Seriously*, Ronald Dworkin's analysis is designed in part to provide a principled method for judicial decision making which could be used by an activist court such as the Warren Court.[80] In a more recent work, *Law's*

Empire, Dworkin continues his conversation with Hart while offering a more advanced understanding of his rights position.[81] Dworkin now disclaims the activist stance while still insisting on the importance of taking rights seriously.[82] For the purposes of understanding the uses of rights it is important to discuss both phases of Dworkin's work. In *Taking Rights Seriously*, Dworkin presents his understanding of rights as trumps[83] and rights as reasons.[84] After a discussion of each use of rights there will be a brief review of the Hart-Dworkin conversation as it had developed at the time *Taking Rights Seriously* was published. Following that, there will be a summary of Dworkin's more advanced and somewhat changed position as presented in *Law's Empire* including some of his further contributions to the conversation with Hart. Although Dworkin has revised his views somewhat, it is important to discuss both his earlier and later thought to offer a wider spectrum of the potential uses of rights.

(i) <u>Rights as Trumps</u>

Ronald Dworkin in *Taking Rights Seriously* and elsewhere speaks of rights as trumps.[85] His assertion that rights are trumps is related to his division of reasons for political decisions into reasons of principle and reasons of policy.[86] Principles are reasons based upon individual right while policies are reasons based upon group goals.[87] It is not necessary to agree with Dworkin that judges ought always to rest their decisions on principle rather than policy to recognize that in our society rights (or principles as reasons based on rights) sometimes and perhaps often trump policies.

While Dworkin claims he is offering a new way of talking about the manner in which judges arrive at and justify decisions[88] he also is prescribing a judicial decision making method. It is not necessary to accept Dworkin's method and to reject a pragmatic-instrumentalist method to recognize that at times rights should trump policies. Robert Summers who has recently offered a theory of the pragmatist-instrumentalist method has expressed admiration for Dworkin's work and has found a role in the theory he offers for moral (or rights based) goals in judicial decision making.[89] It makes sense in most methods that strong rights should trump weak policies. Dworkin should and probably would concede that weak rights should yield to strong policies as in a conflict between rights a strong right will trump a weaker right.[90] The controversial question is whether strong rights should trump strong policies.

H. L. A. Hart describes statements concerning rights as a means of drawing conclusions within a system of rules.[91] Much of Dworkin's analysis in *Taking Rights Seriously* likewise is concerned with systems of rules. When he speaks of rights as trumps he means that it is appropriate to reach that conclusion within a system of rules.[92] However, the rules as H. L. A. Hart recognized are often open-textured.[93] The rules have a clear core meaning where there is general agreement as to their application but are surrounded by a shadowy or penumbral area where the rules may or may not apply.[94] Dworkin is particularly concerned with the great contested moral concepts such as due process of law or cruel and unusual punishment found in the United States Constitution.[95] These concepts also have a core meaning and are surrounded by a penumbral area.[96] Dworkin, in his earlier work, wants courts to take rights seriously when making penumbral area decisions. Under his decision making method it is proper to draw a conclusion in a penumbral area decision on the basis of a theory of government or justice which the particular judge holds or which he believes has the best institutional fit.[97] With the aid of his basic theory a judge should form a conceptualization or theory of the contested moral concept relevant to his decision.[98] Then the judge draws a conclusion as to the rights of the litigants within a system of open-textured rules based ultimately on his basic theory of government or justice.[99]

(ii) Rights as Reasons

Ronald Dworkin in *Taking Rights Seriously* not only describes rights as trumps but also as reasons.[100] His discussion of rights as reasons is related to his distinction between concrete and abstract rights and institutional and background rights.[101] The holding of a judge in a case establishes a concrete right.[102] For example, a judge may find that incarcerating convicted criminals in an overcrowded antiquated prison facility with poor food, poor toilet facilities and inadequate protection against violence is cruel and unusual punishment.[103] The judge's holding establishes a concrete right not to be incarcerated in that or a similar facility. The Eighth Amendment's prohibition of cruel and unusual punishment[104] is a reason for establishing the concrete right found in the judge's holding. In turn, the right not to be subjected to cruel and unusual punishment is an abstract institutional right which is different than the concrete right not to be incarcerated in an inadequate and dangerous facility. The abstract right is a reason for establishing the concrete right.[105] The Eighth Amendment's prohibition of cruel and unusual punishment is properly described as an institutional right since it is found in the United States Constitution. Cruel and unusual, however, is an open-textured contested moral concept.[106] Judges will disagree on its meaning. There will be certain clear core instances on which judges will generally agree and cases where judges will disagree. The latter cases could be described as penumbra area cases which arise in the shadowy area where the contested concept may or may not apply.

Dworkin wants to take rights seriously in penumbra area cases. A judge should not decide these cases on the basis of whim nor on the basis of a policy analysis, that is an analysis of group advantage.[107] Rather the judge should offer an understanding or theory of the contested moral concept which will explain all the cases the judge wants to decide or refrain from overruling under the provision of the Constitution containing that concept.[108] For example, in explaining the Eighth Amendment judges often state that it is designed to advance human dignity and to reflect the evolving standards of human decency.[109] These background rights and concepts form the basis for a theory of the Eighth Amendment and a foundation for deciding hard or penumbral cases.[110]

Dworkin would impose a further requirement: the judge's understanding of various open-textured contested moral concepts in the United States Constitution should be grounded in turn in a consistent theory of government or justice.[111] The judge, for example, should be able to explain human dignity or standards of human decency on the basis of his understanding of justice or rights in general.[112] A consistent general theory which grounds a judge's reasons for his decisions in penumbral area cases guards against decisions based on momentary whim, provides consistency and a basis for predicting the judge's decisions, and ultimately a basis for asserting that those decisions are founded on principle.

Rights, then, in Dworkin's method for judicial decision making, as presented in *Taking Rights Seriously,* serve as reasons for decisions. Concrete rights stated in the holdings of cases are reasons for the court's judgment or disposition of the case.[113] Abstract institutional rights such as the prohibition of cruel and unusual punishment are reasons for establishing concrete rights.[114] Abstract background rights, such as the right to human dignity, are reasons supporting interpretations of abstract institutional rights.[115] These abstract background rights in turn are grounded in a theory of government or justice.[116] Rights as reasons for court decisions will trump policies which offer competing reasons based on arguments of group advantage.[117]

(iii) The Hart-Dworkin Conversation

Dworkin is influenced substantially by H. L. A. Hart. Like Hart he is very concerned with language and in *Taking Rights Seriously* with systems of rules. In "Hard Cases", a chapter of that book,[118] he accepts Hart's understanding of legal rules as open-textured with a clear core meaning on which there is general agreement and a penumbral area where the rule may or may not apply.[119] He differs with Hart on the manner in which judges should make penumbral decisions. Hart would describe judges as deputy legislators who have strong discretion to apply or not apply the rule in penumbral cases.[120] Dworkin would require a judge to decide penumbral area cases on the basis of reasons of principle ultimately grounded in a general theory of justice rather than on the basis of reasons of policy.[121] He argues that a judge so restricted does not have strong discretion to decide on the basis of whatever considerations appeal at the moment.[122] Rather a judge so restricted must take rights seriously in his penumbral area decisions.[123]

Hart's judge as deputy legislator would be free to decide cases in the pragmatic-instrumentalist tradition on the basis of sound policy considerations.[124] Dworkin's judge must allow rights supported by his theory of justice to trump policy arguments.[125] Dworkin's disagreement with Hart which has been the subject of books by both thinkers[126] is occasioned and made necessary by his desire to provide a foundation in a method by which judges reason on the basis of consistent principles for the work of an activist rights oriented court. A large question is whether Dworkin's insights and his attempt to support the Warren Court's work in this manner are compatible in any way with the pragmatic instrumentalist tradition that proved so important in overcoming formalism and advancing earlier twentieth century efforts at law reform.[127]

(iv) Law's Empire

More recently in *Law's Empire,*[128] Dworkin rejects the notion that his theory is designed to support an activist court and the notion that one can distinguish between the core and penumbra of legal concepts.[129] In *Law's Empire*, Dworkin offers an extended argument concerning the role of interpretation and integrity in law. He now rejects Hart's analysis of the open texture of law, the notion of the core and penumbra, on the ground that this is an attempt to discover a hidden but actually unreal semantic theory in the practice of lawyers and courts.[130] Dworkin contends now that law is not represented only by clear acts of past authority such as courts or legislatures which cover a certain precise area (the core) leaving decision makers free to make new law beyond that area because there is no old law.[131] Rather, he would approach problems of clear and disputed law in a similar manner. All legal conclusions result from an interpretation of law both in clear and disputed cases.[132] Dworkin rejects two rival conceptions or theories of law at what he calls the interpretative stage, namely conventionalism[133] and legal pragmatism.[134] In their place he offers his own understanding of law as integrity.[135]

A judge such as Judge Hercules who accepts law as integrity should develop a theory or interpretation of law which has the potential of making all law completely consistent. One can do this only by employing principled reasoning and tracing one's decisions including interpretations of statutes and constitutions to a consistent set of foundational principles, preferably moral principles.[136] These principles should have institutional fit although some old decisions can be discarded under a theory of mistakes.[137] Hercules' principles must interpret our institutions and law and not those of Mars and make the most of them that can be made. The principles which justify old decisions, statutes, and constitutions, past political decisions, become the justification for future decisions in hard cases. Law as integrity then is a theory which takes rights established in the past and the principles which support them very seriously.[138] Dworkin, in *Law's Empire*, offers a theory in which rights as reasons are the central aspect of his understanding of law. The difficulty is that he does not distinguish between fundamental human rights protected by a constitution or major past decisions and other legal rights simply embodied in previous precedent.[139] In *Law's Empire*, Dworkin does not offer a theory of strong rights (which will prevail over all but the most serious competition) and weak rights (which will yield to serious competing considerations). All legal rights are taken with the utmost seriousness.[140]

D. Rights as Goals

Robert Summers has offered recently a theory of pragmatic instrumentalism.[141] He would characterize a number of early twentieth century thinkers, including the followers of sociological jurisprudence and legal realism, as pragmatic instrumentalists.[142] A principal form of reasoning used by judges of this view is what Summers calls means-goal reasoning.[143] The pragmatic-instrumentalist method as described by Summers is probably the dominant form of judicial decision making in America during the mid and later twentieth century. It is important to ask, then, whether its principal technique, means-goal reasoning is at all compatible with principled reasoning as described by Dworkin.

Perhaps one can perceive economic rights as goals more easily than one can so perceive individual or political rights. The following discussion will illustrate rights as goals first in the context of economic rights and then in the context of non-economic constitutional and political rights. Then the inquiry will turn to whether it is possible to take rights seriously if rights are understood as goals.[144]

Understanding rights as societal goals is incompatible with Dworkin's terminology. According to Dworkin's analysis in *Taking Rights Seriously*, principles are reasons for political including judicial decisions which are based on an individual's claim of right.[145] In contrast policies are reasons based on group goals.[146] To Dworkin societal goals would support policies but would not of themselves be principles or reasons based on right.[147] In view of the use by others of language describing rights as goals Dworkin's analysis may not be satisfactory. In *Law's Empire,* Dworkin attacks Pragmatism broadly defined as an appropriate interpretation of our legal system.[148] It is not clear and certainly doubtful that his or Judge Hercules' interpretation of the task of adjudication would have any role for means-goal reasoning.

(i) Economic Rights as Goals

The Universal Declaration of Human Rights [149] proclaimed by the United Nations General Assembly states rights in the form of goals to be achieved. The document offers "a common standard of achievement for all peoples and all nations" who shall "strive by teaching and education to promote respect for these rights and freedoms and by progressive measures, national and international, to secure their universal and effective recognition and observance...".[150] The Declaration treats personal liberties such "the right to life, liberty and security of person"[151] and freedom from "arbitrary arrest, detention or exile" as goals.[152] However, it may be that economic rights such as those stated in Articles 22 and 23 may be more easily perceived as goals to be achieved. Article 22 states:

> Everyone, as a member of society, has the right to social security and is entitled to realization, through national effort and international co-operation and in accordance with the organization and resources of each State, of the economic, social and cultural rights indispensable for his dignity and the free development of his personality.[153]

National effort and international cooperation may be limited by the resources available. The resources necessary to establish social security may be developed over time but may not be available instantaneously. The right to social security is a goal to be pursued as is the right to an appropriate standard of living as described in Article 25 which states in part:

> 1. Everyone has the right to a standard of living adequate for the health and well being of himself and of his family, including food, clothing, housing and medical care...[154]

The right to an adequate standard of living is not a trump in the Dworkin sense. A holding of a court could not direct that X and all persons like him be given an adequate standard of living. In an underdeveloped country, for example, the resources to afford X and those like him an adequate standard of living may not be present. Due to transportation and like difficulties outside resources supplied by willing nations may not be sufficient to supplement adequately the poor resources of the underdeveloped nation. The right to an adequate standard of living is a goal to be pursued but not a trump which can sweep aside instantaneously all competing considerations.

One should note the important discussion over the priority of economic as opposed to political and individual rights. There are those who would contend that economic rights are goals which should be pursued even if it is necessary to trample on individual and political rights in order to do so.[155] John Rawls offers an interesting way of ordering the priority of rights.[156] His first principle of justice protects individual and some political rights. It states: "each person is to have an equal right to the most extensive basic liberty compatible with a similar liberty for others."[157] The second principle of justice addresses economic as well as political rights. It states: "social and economic inqualities are to be arranged so that they are both (a) reasonably expected to be to everyone's advantage, and (b) attached to positions and offices open to all."[158] Rawls offers his understanding of lexical ordering as a way of determining the priority of the individual rights protected by his first principle and the economic rights protected by the second principle.[159] The first principle is lexically prior to the second principle.[160] Rights under the second principle should be protected only when the first principle is not violated.[161]

(ii) <u>Constitutionally Protected Individual and Political Rights as Goals:</u>

Those whom Summers describes as pragmatic instrumentalists[162] and whom others describe as followers of sociological jurisprudence or legal realism tended to describe law as a means to achievement of social goals. One reason for their attack on formalism was the failure of formalist judges to relate law to social goals or policies.[163] The pragmatic instrumentalists characteristically would take a more extreme position that law is only a means.[164] Summers finds that these thinkers and others have neglected the problem of choice of goals as well as analysis of the different forms of means-goal relationships.[165] Neglect of the choice of goals problem may have been justified by the predominant pragmatic instrumentalist value theory. Summers explains "that the primary tenet of the instrumentalist theory of value was that law should seek to maximize the realization of existing wants and interests."[166] In the view of some pragmatists the only reason for recognizing a claim is that it is made.[167] The task of the law then is to reconcile competing claims in such a way that effect and recognition can be given to as many as possible.[168]

The value theory just described tends to avoid and conceal the problem of choice between goals. Indeed because a multiplicity of specific decisions must be made in the process of applying and reconciling rules promoting social goals judges may make hidden choices between goals while denying that they are choosing and insisting that they are attempting to advance all existing wants and needs. Instrumentalists, such as Llewellyn, accused formalist judges of making hidden choices in a similar manner while insisting that they simply were applying the law.[169] Summers would find compatible with his thought Dworkin's desire for a general theory of government or justice that, using pragmatic-instrumentalist method, would become the basis for choice between social goals when such a choice was permitted by the leeways or penumbral areas of legal rules.[170]

Under a theory of democratic government, equality including racial equality could be considered an important social goal. The equal protection clause of the Fourteenth Amendment[171] under such a theory would be an institutional validation of that goal and an attempt to advance it. The Supreme Court in *Plessy v. Ferguson*[172] arguably thought that separate but equal school facilities were an adequate means for achieving the social goal of equality.[173] The Warren Court in *Brown v. Board of Education*[174] after examining social science studies rejected this means for achieving racial equality.[175]

The same Court in *New York Times v. Sullivan*[176] provides another example of means-goal reasoning. In that case, Georgia law enforcement officials sued the New York Times for a libel allegedly published in an advertisement paid for by supporters of Dr. Martin Luther King.[177] The advertisement criticized Georgia law enforcement and apparently contained some false statements of fact.[178] The Supreme Court held that the First Amendment protection of freedom of the press required modification of the common law action in libel. To recover the plaintiff must show in addition to the traditional elements of libel that the newspaper acted maliciously, that is with knowledge that its statements were false or with reckless disregard of the truth.[179] The Supreme Court supported its holding by noting the tradition of robust political discussion in the United States and our commitment to such robust discussion as a means of discovering the truth.[180] Under a theory of democratic government the role for the First Amendment protection of freedom of the press could be to advance the role of robust discussion which in turn would allow an informed citizenry to make sensible choices in governing themselves. Freedom of the press is a means serving the goal of informed choice in democratic government. Modifying the libel laws is a means for advancing the social goal of freedom of the press and the more ultimate social goals served by a free press.

Brown v. Board of Education[181] and *New York Times v. Sullivan*[182] offer examples of court holdings designed to advance individual and political rights as social goals. Equality is better advanced by desegregation than by separate but equal facilities. Freedom of the press and robust discussion can be promoted by modifying the libel laws. While the Court could have supported both decisions by reference to a democratic theory of government, it refrained from offering this justification.

The Warren Court's decisions, particularly *Brown v. Board of Education*[183] were attacked precisely because they were justified by means-goal reasoning with an emphasis upon discussion of means rather than by principled reasoning.[184] An important question which must be posed, then, is whether means-goal reasoning can adequately support an assertion of rights.

(iii) <u>If Rights are Goals is it Possible to take Rights Seriously?</u>

In the present age of theory when a Dworkin seeks to underpin the activist struggles of the Warren Court with a theoretical foundation,[185] and a Summers following to some extent in the footsteps of Hart[186] attempts to set in order the insights of sociological jurisprudence and legal realists,[187] perhaps we should turn to the work of theorists to answer the question just posed. We should be a little reluctant to do so because the efforts of the theorist when applied to the practical work of law reformers is a little bit like Aunt Sally's attempt to civilize Huck Finn.[188] Reform minded thinkers and judges may act like Huck in response to our efforts and threaten to retreat to the "Indian Territory".[189]

Dworkin insists that principles as reasons based on individual rights should be the typical basis for judicial decisions[190] and should trump policies that are reasons based upon group, state, or national goals.[191] In *Brown v. Board of Education*[192] the Warren Court rejected separate but equal facilities primarily because they were not an adequate means of achieving the goal of racial equality. In contrast, one could following Dworkin's method develop a conceptualization or theory of equality or of the concept of equal protection in the Fourteenth Amendment.[193] Then, one could find that separate although supposedly equal facilities were logically inconsistent with the notion of equality or equal protection as explained by one's theory. This analysis would not require an examination of whether separate but equal facilities adequately served the goal of establishing racial equality. Dworkin's method offers a response to those critics of the Warren Court who insisted upon principled reasoning[194] and hence offers a challenge to understanding rights as goals.[195]

In response one can offer at least two recent theoretical developments: (i) Summers' suggestion that a theory of government or justice could provide the foundation for choosing between goals[196] and (ii) Rawls'use of the method of lexically ordering the rights protected by his two principles of justice.[197]

Summers' suggestion makes it possible to anchor goal rights in a fundamental theory or commitment[198] rather than simply in a practical or reform minded response to felt needs of the moment. Under a fundamental theory some goal rights may trump competing policies. While further development of his suggestion is necessary, Summers' insight[199] may offer the beginnings of a model of rights which could compete with Dworkin's understanding.

Rawls' method of lexically ordering rights would offer a judge the opportunity to insist that certain individual and political rights should prevail over competing economic rights.[200] He could nevertheless insist that economic goal rights are rights properly so called and that such rights prevail on appropriate occasions over competing policies.[201] Perhaps Rawls' lexical ordering of individual and economic rights may be more useful than Dworkin's distinction between principles and policies.

Both the pragmatic-instrumentalists described by Summers, and Rawls in his second principle of justice would be open to talking about group rights as well as individual rights. Indeed one can contemplate discussion of such national rights as the right of an underdeveloped country to economic progress. Typically group rights are goal rights.[202] However, if one accepts the notion of rights as goals, it becomes necessary to distinguish between these and other competing goals which one would not classify as rights. Developing that distinction will be one of the tasks of the latter portions of this book.[203]

(iv) Goals, Rights, and Other Recent Pragmatists

Judge Richard Posner concludes his book, *The Problems of Jurisprudence*,[204] with a Chapter 15 entitled, "A Pragmatist Manifesto."[205] There he notes the current revival of pragmatism:

> beginning in the 1960s with the waning of logical positivism, pragmatism came charging back in the person of Richard Rorty, followed in the 1970s by critical legal studies--the radical child of legal realism--and in the 1980s by a school of legal neopragmatists, including some feminists.[206]

Posner's brand of pragmatist which is well within the mainstream would be incompatible with Summer's proposal as described above[207] because it rejects foundations and overarching theory. It would, of course, be incompatible with and would reject as not useful the form of interpretation proposed by Dworkin in *Law's Empire*.[208]

Nevertheless, Posner places considerable emphasis on means-goals reasoning which he considers an important form of practical reason.[209] In the usual run of cases, Judge Posner would give considerable weight to ordinary legal reasoning and to what Dworkin would consider legal rights. While Posner does not believe that that form of reasoning reaches ultimate "truth" or perhaps what Dworkin would call the one right answer it does not appear that he simply pays lip service to "legal rights" or acts "as if" they were rights to use Dworkin's terminology when attacking pragmatism.[210] Posner also places considerable emphasis on his oath to support the Constitution which would appear to support a rights theory, although a rights theory written in small letters.[211]

Without an overarching theory, then, a judge nevertheless may perceive normal legal rights and important constitutional rights as goals or as means to the achievement of goals. In the ordinary decision of cases, he readily may analyze rights in terms of means-goals reasoning and reach conclusions on the basis of that analysis. From the point of view of an external observer or a practicing attorney, one could predict fairly that the pragmatist judge of the Posner vintage would treat certain rights as goals and others as means and afford remedies on the basis of that analysis. It also appears that the pragmatist judge is employing means-end reasoning to draw conclusions within the legal system or the system of legal reasoning (the Common Law Tradition) as he understands it. Rights as goals, and Rights as means then may be Rights as Remedies and Rights as conclusions.

E. Rights as Claims; Rights as Criticism

H. L. A. Hart describes rights as conclusions drawn

within a system of rules by way ruling, claim, or criticism.[212] In addition to the system of rules there are three distinct points of view, roles, or what Llewellyn describes as law jobs[213] referred to in that analysis. The judge or other official makes a ruling. A litigant or his attorney may make a claim. A social reformer or a scholar may criticize a court decision without making a claim. There are other relevant points of view from the perspective of other law jobs. A planning attorney or one counseling Holmes' bad man will make a prediction for planning or counseling purposes of what the courts are likely to do.[214] Later in the book there will be further discussion of rights as seen from the points of view of various law jobs.[215] Point of view analysis may offer one basis for understanding the differing perspectives from which various thinkers use the language of rights and hence one possible way of reconciling contrasting uses.

Hart would describe a claim of right or a criticism of a statement concerning rights as a conclusion drawn within a system of rules.[216] Other systems may be imagined and other thinkers may perceive rights within the context of other systems. A system of ethical, political, or religious beliefs may or may not be a system of rules. In any event, one may be able to arrive at conclusions within a system of ethical, political, or religious beliefs. A right then may be a conclusion arrived at within a system of ethical, political, or religious beliefs. Rawls offers a Theory of Justice. A right may be a conclusion drawn within his Theory of Justice.[217] Rawls' Theory is an example of the sort of general theory of government or justice which Dworkin would require of a judge using his decision making method.[218] Under that method, then, a right is not only a conclusion drawn within a system of rules but in penumbral area cases is a conclusion drawn within the theory of government or justice. Using Hart's analysis a right is a conclusion drawn within these various systems not only by way of ruling but also by way of claim or criticism.

This broadening and development of Hart's analysis will be helpful in the subsequent discussion of rights as political resources. Rights may become political resources when arrived at as conclusions within political or other systems. Rights as conclusions which become political resources may be stated in rulings, claims, or criticism.

F. Rights as Resources

Stuart Scheingold in his *Politics of Rights*[219] describes rights as political resources. A judicial decision, according to Scheingold, is an official declaration that the right recognized in the decision is a goal of public policy.[220] Scheingold would tend to perceive rights as goals but as subordinate goals. If one examines our political system rather than more narrowly discussing the legal system, it will be found that "our rights are always at risk in the political arena"[221] because laws, as well as judges, "are delivered to us by the dominant political coalition".[222] Nevertheless our political system "is responsive to constitutional values - albeit imperfectly and circuitously"[223] and indeed litigation can be of some help in promoting rights.[224] Scheingold, then, as a conclusion from his examination of the power relationships in our political system, puts before us a modified rule skepticism.

While change in our political system cannot be "based exclusively on rights"[225] nevertheless one can use rights to promote political activation, organization and mobilization. Rights are "a political resource which can be deployed, primarily through litigation, to spark hopes and indignation".[226] Legal tactics should not be developed or "judged in isolation" from the strategy of political mobilization.[227]

The use of legal tactics in political mobilization is made possible by what Scheingold calls the "myth of rights".[228] The myth of rights is an American ideology derived from values and symbols of legitimacy found in American law. "The myth of rights provides political *ideals*" that "are reflected in the formal *rules* which structure American institutions" and "influence the *behavior* of governmental officials and private citizens."[229] As a picture of reality the myth is misleading in some respects. American political institutions are not as "regularly responsive to constitutional values"[230] as portrayed by the myth of rights. As a modified rule skeptic Scheingold doubts that litigation and judicial decisions produce regular and rapid changes in the political power structure. Nevertheless the myth of rights and its acceptance in America provide the psychological foundation for the use of rights as political resources. "The principal impact of the myth of rights is on cognition and, more specifically, on perceptions of legitimacy."[231] In turn:

> Political behavior is regularly cued and shaped by perception. Belief in the law, acceptance of constitutional values, respect for legal institutions -- these all become political facts, albeit with contradictory implications.[232]

Scheingold, then, advises activist lawyers to coordinate litigation with the political activities of the interest groups which they represent.[233] As in the great campaign of the NAACP which culminated in *Brown v. Board of Education*[234] the claim of right and ultimately the recognition of right by a court can serve to mobilize the group, gather adherents and allies, and discourage opponents.[235] As well as securing to some extent the advantages protected by the right claimed and ultimately declared the general interests of the group are advanced by litigation claiming and seeking to enforce rights.

H. L. A. Hart is concerned with the language and structure of the legal system while Stuart Scheingold examines the political system. Nevertheless there are similarities in their approaches and insights. Unlike Dworkin, Hart is attempting to describe a legal system rather than prescribing a decision making method for judges. Typically Hart offers great clarifying concepts designed to illumine our difficulties in understanding and describing a legal system. Scheingold likewise is engaged largely in description rather than prescription although he has good advice for activist lawyers.[236] However, what Scheingold describes is the political rather than the legal system. He is attempting to locate the role of legal rights and litigation regarding them in the political system.[237]

An important aspect of the political system as Scheingold describes it is the myth of rights.[238] Given the myth of rights some of Hart's insights can be employed to develop Scheingold's analysis. When the political behavior of the American public ultimately changes to accommodate a court declared right one reason for the change lies in the ideological realm. A conclusion has been drawn within the myth of rights that the particular right in question is legitimate.[239] Indeed as in Dworkin's analysis a fundamental theory, here an ideology, the myth of rights, provides an ultimate reason for acceptance of the right declared by the courts. When an interest group sponsoring litigation or otherwise claims a right not yet declared by a court it is appealing to the myth of rights and attempting to expand our perception of the myth sufficiently to accommodate the interest it is supporting. When American public opinion ultimately changes to accommodate a court declared right one reason for the change lies in the ideological realm. A conclusion has been drawn within the myth of rights, namely, the right claimed. The interest group by way of claim is drawing a conclusion and encouraging others to draw the same conclusion within the myth of rights which is an aspect of the political system.[240] The group could also criticize and attack political stances and judicial decisions on the basis of conclusions which the group claims as legitimate within the myth of rights. One may conclude, then, that in that portion of politics, called by Scheingold the politics of rights, rights are conclusions drawn with the help of other political tools within the ideological system called the myth of rights. These conclusions are drawn as in Hart's analysis of the legal system as rulings, claims or criticisms. Interest groups use the politics of rights to criticize others and to make claims upon others in the political system. Legal rights and the language of legal rights are tools for communicating and gaining advantages through that communication in the political system.[241]

G. Crits (Rights as Ideology?)

In his Kharas lecture, "The Bork Nomination and American Constitutional History," Morton Horwitz contrasts two views of the Constitution at stake in the Bork hearings.[242] The first which he favors perceives a living Constitution whose meaning changes with the times[243] perhaps in response to what Holmes called the "felt necessities"[244] or perhaps in response to political power. The second supported, Horwitz contended, somewhat naively by Senator Biden, was the idea that the Constitution protected certain inalienable rights.[245] Horwitz perceived these two understandings of constitutional law as being inconsistent and in conflict:

> But in any event, these two strands, that of a living changeable constitution and that of inalienable rights, have marched through American history in permanent conflict, although often attempting to accommodate themselves to each other.[246]

Horwitz had considerable problems with the rights oriented understanding of the Constitution. He noted: "in 1937 virtually all progressive legal thinkers were hostile to the idea of rights."[247] In regard to "the eternal character of rights"[248] reaffirmed by Senator Biden he commented: "[t]he question is therefore whether any sophisticated person in the twentieth century could really believe that."[249] He concluded: "[t]he history of rights for 150 years of our constitutional history has basically been the doctrine of the wealthy and powerful. It is only in the last 50 years that this has changed."[250] He then, asked: "[i]s that a fundamental change? Is that a permanent change?"[251]

In his "An Essay on Rights" in the Texas Law Review Symposium on Rights,[252] Mark Tushnet takes a similarly critical view of rights discourse. He, too, argues that "[t]he use of rights in contemporary discourse impedes advances by progressive social forces, which I call the 'party of humanity'."[253] Like Horwitz, he attacks "the eternal character of rights," particularly in the abstract, pointing out that slight changes in the structure of society would render a number of claims concerning specific rights implausible.[254] Rights discourse rather is about what structure one desires for a specific society and what specific rights will promote that structure. "The conditions of the society define exactly what kind of rights-talk makes sense, [and that] in turn defines what the society is."[255] He notes that in rights discourse: "[f]undamental indeterminacy occurs because rights have a social context."[256] Rather than using rights discourse one should argue about what sort of society we should have. In that argument rights discourse creates obstacles for the party of humanity because "the predominance of negative rights creates an ideological barrier to the extension of positive rights in our culture."[257] Negative rights are restraints ("to be free from interference")[258] while positive rights are "to have various things."[259] In other words, negative rights which predominate in our culture restrain the ideological reshaping of society and hence hinder the cause of the party of humanity.

One can find a similar critique of the present use of rights in Roberto Unger's article, "The Critical Legal Studies Movement."[260] For example, he contends:

> The established system of rights presents another, less familiar obstacle to the aims of this institutional program: the absence of legal principles and entitlements capable of informing communal life--those areas of social existence where people stand in a relationship of heightened mutual vulnerability and responsibility toward each other. For one thing, our dominant conception of right imagines the right as a zone of discretion of the rightholder, a zone whose boundaries are more or less rigidly fixed at the time of the initial definition of the right. The right is a loaded gun that the rightholder may shoot at will in his corner of town. Outside that corner the other licensed gunmen may shoot him down. But the give-and-take of communal life and its characteristic concern for the actual effect of any decision upon the other person are incompatable with this view of right and therefore, if this is the only possible view, with any regime of rights.[261]

Like Tushnet, Unger is concerned with the restraints which a regime of rights imposes on the reshaping of society in a more communitarian direction. Earlier it was noted that Unger would use rights, such as destabilization rights, in his reshaped society to promote ideological goals.[262] Common themes in Horwitz, Tushnet, and Unger, are the apparent and erroneous "eternal nature of rights," the use of rights in the service of ideology, including contrary to the cause of humanity to protect current establishment interests, and the importance of talking rather about the structure which society should have.[263] Unger and Duncan Kennedy would use rights to restructure society and in that new society to promote ideological goals.

It is worth comparing and contrasting the Crits and Ronald Dworkin. Like the Crits, Dworkin wants to talk about what society should look like. At one level he requires Judge Hercules to offer a theory of government or justice. In contrast to the Crits, Hercules' theory is required to have institutional fit and to be an interpretation of existing societal structures and constitutional provisions. His method for judicial decision making affords a method by which judges of differing views representing perhaps great opposing theories of society can enter into conversation with each other in the course of judicial decision making and constitutional interpretation. In other words, rights discourse as perceived by Dworkin would be precisely about the structure which society should have.[264] It would, of course, be a more limited discussion than that envisioned by the Crits because it would be confined to interpretations of existing structures and provisions. On a higher level, however, Dworkin is offering a major contending theory about the structure which society should have. Briefly, society should be one in which all persons are afforded equal respect and concern. Rights have an important role in that structure as protections for equal respect and concern and hence as restraints upon power, including the power to reshape society in ways which would violate equal respect and concern.[265] Dworkin's fundamental theory of society may be at odds with that of the Crits but it is a fair question, which is more in accord with the cause of humanity. Dworkin is overly rigid in his theory of rights; Judge Hercules,once he has established his theory of government or justice is required to make decisions consistent with it and is not allowed readily to change his theory.[266] However, Dworkin opposes the same originalist notions of constitutional rights that Horwitz attacks and his theory of constitutional interpretation could not be described as originalist.[267] Perhaps Senator Biden had in mind something like Dworkin's method of interpretation when he defended the Declaration of Independence and the rights approach to constitutional decision making.[268]

The comparison between the understanding of rights in the Critical Legal Studies Movement and Scheingold's theory of the Politics of Rights and his use of rights as resources to promote interests[269] is also worth making and perhaps obvious. Many Crits, however, would think that Scheingold's use of rights as resources ultimately would be counterproductive for the left or the cause of humanity.

Feminist[270] and Outsider Jurisprudence[271] could be perceived as specialized developments from the Critical Legal Studies Movement. If these recent schools are so understood, then, they share many of the insights and views of the Crits as described above. They, too, would perceive rights in the context of current establishment economic and social interests and as means to promote present establishment ideological positions. They, too, would want to talk about what structure society should have. One proposal would center on the concept of a Caring Society.[272] They, too, would use rights perhaps as Scheingold suggests to promote feminist or outsider interests or in a restructured society to promote ideological goals.

For historical reasons, one may treat Feminist and Outsider Jurisprudence as versions of Critical Legal Studies since the later definitely influenced and perhaps inspired the former. That historical understanding, however, may be too confining and may distort important differences. One important difference will be mentioned in the next part in the discussion of rights as rhetoric, where rights discourse may be used among other functions as a means of sharing human experience.[273]

H. Rights As Rhetoric

Like the Crits, James Boyd White imagines those engaged in legal argument ideally talking about what shape our society ought to have.[274] Perhaps unlike the Crits he perceives that discussion occuring in a societal and cultural context. The Crits surely would agree that legal arguments are made in a cultural context. White, however, sees that context as more constraining. For example,

> For me it follows that the law is best regarded not as a kind of social science but as one of the humanities. Its practice requires a constant sense of the resources and limits of one's language and culture; a conscious attention to the silence against which all language action takes place, to what *cannot* be said; an awareness of one's own need for an education, particularly for an education from the past that has created our linguistic and intellectual inheritance; a recognition that it is our responsibility to preserve and to improve this inheritance leaving it fit for use

> by others; an acknowledgement that the authority of this inheritance is at once real and tentative; and an awareness that others, who are all also users of language, composers of texts, and members of communities, are entitled to basic respect as autonomous and equal persons. All these things mark it as an essentially practical and literary, rather than scientific or theoretical activity.[275]

Within this context the lawyer exercises the art of persuasion or rhetoric. Part of the argument which constitutes society and holds it together is a dispute over appropriate forms of persuasion. In his first chapter, White offers a play by Sophocles, the Philoctetes, as a context[276] in which to discuss two forms of persuasion, the trickery or deception practiced by Odysseus, and the sharing of human experience "that recognizes the autonomy, worth and liberty of the other"[277] from time to time employed by Neoptolamus. In his "A Dialogue on the Ethics of Argument", Chapter 10 of the book,[278] White offers reflections on the choice of forms of argument and justification for the lawyer's role. In regard to the sharing of experiences, he remarks through one of the characters in the dialogue:

> the law as I describe it becomes a repository of shared experiences, a set of experiments and trials and failures, which are by the law made intelligible and sharable. This is a culture of experience and experiment; This means that the law is a way in which the community defines itself, not once and for all, but over and over, and in the process educates itself about its own character and the nature of the world.[279]

White's vision of a community in which persons are related to each other by the rhetoric of argument which constitutes and reconstitutes society surely includes the uses of rights described in this book. The various uses of rights could be perceived as rhetoric and as principal tools in that argument which constitutes and reconstitutes community and through which persons are related to each other. In other words, rights are significant means by which persons establish, change, talk about, fight about, reconcile and struggle with human relations. As the Crits emphasize there may be bad and unconscionable uses of the rhetoric of rights. Among other problems the crafty and tricky Odysseus is always with us. Nevertheless the arguments about rights are important ways in which persons are related to each other and society is constituted.

White's vision could benefit from Dworkin's analysis and vice versa. Dworkin takes the point of view of a judge while White regularly discusses law from the perspective of the practicing attorney, particularly the litigating attorney engaged in argument. While Dworkin overlooks the ongoing nature of the argument and the relation between persons established by it, White touches only tangentally on the philosophical foundations of the judge's interpretation of society, its institutions and the law. Together Dworkin's fundamental principle, afford all persons equal respect and concern,[280] and White's vision of a society of equal and autonomous persons related by argument over the constitution of society[281] could offer a powerful understanding of persons and their relation to law. That understanding should not overlook the Politics of law and rights which as Scheingold[282] and the Crits perceive,[283] is one way of relating persons who are only peripherally participating to the main stream of the argument over the constitution of society.

Feminist[284] and Outsider[285] jurisprudence can be understood in the context of White's description of law as rhetoric, or rather his vision of a society composed of equal and autonomous persons related by argument over that society's constitution and reconstitution. Rights, as rhetoric in the context of such a society, could be perceived as a means of sharing feminist or outsider experience and as a tool of advocacy for the reconstitution of society, for example, as a Caring Society. Rights seen as a means for sharing experience or for calling attention to what has been overlooked by society would serve a somewhat different function than rights as tools for the promotion of ideological goals.

Rights, of course, are not the exclusive means for sharing experience or calling attention to oppression. Narration, the telling of stories, offers an alternate means for accomplishing that. Recently, Robin West has suggested that narration and rights discourse should be used alternately or perhaps together for those purposes.[286]

In the context of the sharing of human experience a new model of rights discourse can be offered. Offering that model will be the function of the next chapter of this book.

Chapter III

Horizons, Point of View and a New Model for Rights Discourse

A. Introduction

The purpose of this chapter of the book is to offer a new model or understanding of rights discourse in which rights can be perceived as being used to establish, change, talk about, fight about, reconcile and struggle with human relations. Two clarifying concepts, horizon[287] and point of view analysis,[288] will be helpful in developing a new model of rights discourse and a portion of the discussion will concentrate on each. The grand conversation of twentieth century legal philosophy traced in the last chapter offered a series of different understandings of rights, including the Critical Legal Studies attack on rights. Having followed that conversation one should find it difficult to accept a simple model of rights, for example any of the particular views of rights offered by the participants in the conversation including the party crashers. Any sophisticated model of rights must account for each of these views and for the problems which the Crits properly have found with rights discourse. Horizon and point of view analysis will enable us to offer a model of rights discourse which will account for some of the crits' insights and for the understandings of rights offered by each of the other participants in the grand conversation. We must start, then, with an elucidation of the concept of horizons which will be followed by a discussion of point of view analysis.

B. Horizons

(i) Elucidation of the concept, horizons

Most of us during our lives have entered new horizons.[289] Professional training has provided us with new perceptions and new ways of looking at problems. One way of recognizing the phenomenon of horizons is to cross from one horizon to another. One way of crossing horizons and one occasion for experiencing the phenomenon is to go through a process of training or learning. Imagine for example a young man from a primitive mountain village wandering down to the seaside where he finds and is adopted by a fishing village. In the early weeks following his arrival he will find much that is unfamiliar, strange and unclear to him. However, after living in the village and being trained as a fisherman he will understand much that was puzzling on his arrival. By acquiring lived experience and going through a process of training he will have crossed from the horizon of the mountain hunting village to that of the seaside fishing community.[290] He will have experienced, understood, and to some extent shared the mores of both groups.

Literally the word horizon refers to the circle at the limit of our vision where earth and sky appear to meet. It is the circle of points beyond which we cannot see although from experience we know that objects lie beyond our vision.[291] Intellectually horizons are established by our background and experience, by our culture, our religion, our politics and the like. Horizons are the product of past achievement and affect our range of interests, the matters which we understand, and those which we are curious about.[292] Perhaps the questions which we normally ask and pursue mark the usual limits of our horizons.[293] While we know that other questions can be asked they do not interest us and we would be unfamiliar to some degree with the answers. Intellectually, the horizons established by our culture, background, training and the questions we ask mark the ordinary limits of our understanding and interest.

A familiar example is that of an animal biologist and a botanist walking together across a country field. The botanist will look for, notice, and remark upon the varied vegetable life abounding in the field while the biologist will be concerned more with the hidden animal life or perhaps with the more persistently obvious insects. The ability to see, understand, and explain events in the country field may depend upon the questions which one asks or which one is accustomed to ask. It may also depend on the methodology which one uses or is trained to use. In this way horizons are established by one's methodology and by the questions which one asks.[294]

A person of experience may be familiar with multiple horizons. He may have worked at a number of jobs, traveled widely (knowing the horizons, for example, of both San Francisco and New York) or have been trained in dual professions. A judge may be an economist as well as a lawyer. He may be able to ask questions related to economics as well as law.[295] In addition he may have horizons established by his mid-western youth, by his religious experience, his political campaigns and his philosophical positions. "Horizons then are the sweep of our interests and of our knowledge; they are the fertile source of further knowledge and care; but they also are the boundaries that limit our capacities for assimilating more than we already have attained."[296]

(ii) Horizons, Obligation and Legal Decision Making

Just as one's intellectual horizons may be limited or expanded by one's experience, training, method of inquiry and the like so one's moral horizons may be limited or more inclusive because of the way one was brought up, because of the political interests that one has, one's understanding or acceptance of religion, one's moral theory or lack thereof and the like. The understanding that a judge has of government, law and justice shares the characteristics of moral understanding. The judge's ability to understand or appreciate legal arguments including those based upon claims or theories of justice will be limited by the judge's political, social and cultural background by his legal experience and by his theory of government or justice.

However, just as one can cross intellectual horizons so one can acquire or become familiar with new moral horizons. Young persons of narrow background or upbringing often acquire new moral horizons while attending college. Immigration from the United States to Mexico could expand one's moral horizons. An important or vital experience can break down walls of prejudice or lack of understanding. The experience of the Holocaust changed the moral outlook of many. Learning a powerful new theory, such as Rawls' Theory of Justice, or the disciplined study of moral philosophy or theology can change or expand one's horizons.[297] After a change of horizons one may accept or understand moral arguments which one would have rejected or failed to appreciate before the change.

A judge with narrow intellectual, moral, and legal horizons may reject a claim of right supported by moral arguments or arguments from justice which he does not understand. Arguably this is what happened in a number of lower Southern court decisions regarding segregation both before and after *Brown v. Board of Education.*[298] One can imagine a judge committed to law and order who simply cannot understand that the police are using *Terry v. Ohio*[299] stops and frisks to harrass members of a Spanish speaking minority. Perhaps the normal behavior of the members of that community appears that of a criminal and suspect type to both the police and a judge. Even a broadly educated judge with wide understanding may fail to appreciate an important claim of right when based on the customs, traditions and needs of a minority community. Since such a judge does not understand the claim of right he does not perceive an obligation to recognize it. From the judge's perspective X does not have a right because Y, the judge, does not perceive an obligation to establish it.

In a complex society the conflicts between submores may present a threat to stability which cannot be resolved through the court system (or other legal institutions) because the relevant judges (or others) are unable to understand claims of right arising from needs, customs or theories in a subculture which is foreign to them. On the other hand, judges with the ability to cross horizons may contribute by their decisions to the stability of society when there is a conflict between submores.

(iii) Transcending and Crossing Horizons

For the purpose of further discussion it may be helpful to distinguish transcending and crossing horizons.[300] Crossing and transcending horizons are similar because by doing either, one acquires a new or broader horizon.[301] One can transcend former horizons perhaps established by political, cultural, or social background by acquiring a higher viewpoint through professional training, by carefully thinking through and accepting a theory of justice, by deepening one's moral perspective or the like.[302] The acquisition of a higher viewpoint does not necessarily change one's former positions. A deeper moral perspective or a theory of justice may provide a more substantial justification or a systematization of one's already accepted positions. A member of a subculture who is trained as an attorney may retain the submores of his culture while being able to express those positions in legal language. A higher viewpoint, however, may compel one to recognize and attempt to understand competing positions while retaining one's own original positions.[303] A deeper moral understanding, a theory of justice or professional training offers that possibility. An attorney from a subculture who becomes a judge may perceive an obligation of fairness or an obligation to adhere to the law when adjudicating a dispute between someone from his subculture and a person from another. However, the perception of that obligation of fairness does not necessarily lead to an understanding of the foreign subculture and its submores.[304] For that the judge must cross horizons by undertaking a process of learning about the strange subculture and its mores.[305]

A judge may perceive an obligation to transcend or cross horizons. When an attorney becomes a judge he may perceive new obligations from his role and from his legal training including an obligation of fairness. Having accepted an obligation of fairness he may act fairly towards persons, for example those accused of crime, whom he attacked vigorously in his former role of prosecutor and for whom he continues to have a distaste. A judge with a strong background in political science or sociology or with great patriotism may articulate a vigorous concern for the stability of society and on that account may determine to transcend and attempt to cross horizons when adjudicating disputes between conflicting submores. A judge on the basis of his moral commitments or his theory of justice may perceive an obligation to afford all persons deep respect and concern and by reason of that commitment a derivative obligation to transcend and cross horizons. One problem with Dworkin's ideal judge, Hercules, is that he has not undertaken the herculean task of crossing horizons and has no place in his method for decision making for the methods of crossing horizons.[306]

In a previous article I contended:

> A judge who wants to take rights seriously will provide means in his decision making methodology for both transcending and crossing horizons. Horizons are established by various processes for learning, by the devices and techniques which accompany these processes, and by the information and ways of acting which are the results of their use. Horizons can be transcended or crossed by using similar learning processes to establish new, different, or more encompassing horizons and may be accompanied by techniques for restraining the vision-blocking characteristics of one's present horizons.[307]

Basically, then, one crosses or transcends horizons in the same way one originally acquires them.[308] Often a common sense process of inquiry and learning is the best way of crossing horizons.[309] The young man from the mountain village described above learned the mores of the fishing village by living there and training as a fisherman. Lord Mansfield deliberately undertook to learn the customs of merchants by dining with them, questioning them, and using them as jurors in merchantile cases.[310] In a similar manner a modern judge "whose practice was largely in negligence law may seek out the sense of a commercial situation"[311] in the following ways:

> Ideally he would acquire that sense through a period of experience with commercial problems and those involved in them. Like Lord Mansfield he would cultivate the acquaintance of merchants and learn from them. In other words he would reproduce deliberately, albeit in a more limited way, the lived experience of the commercial lawyer. In the actual flow of a court's work, however, that careful cultivation of commercial experience may be difficult. As a substitute a skilled judge with the aid of experienced and knowledgeable advocates who are commercial lawyers may acquire the sense of a commercial situation from briefs and oral argument. By descriptions of behavior patterns those briefs and oral arguments may in a limited and vicarious way carry the judge through a lived learning experience with a group or industry."[312]

A judge committed to stability in society or to respect and concern for all persons may use similar learning techniques to work his way into different horizons and experience when adjudicating conflicts between submores. If he does, some Xs will have rights which they would not have had if Y the judge had not undertaken the task of crossing horizons.

Dworkin, in *Law's Empire* and in *Taking Rights Seriously*, has insisted upon an obligation of rigorous consistency in judicial decision making which will lock Judge Hercules within his horizon and prevent him from taking rights seriously in the sense just described.[313]

The Crits are aware of the problem Dworkin has ignored and base much of their criticisms of rights on an awareness that rights (supposedly objective and neutral) are normally perceived within horizons.[314] Nevertheless, they too would fail to take rights seriously in the sense just described (and they may rejoice in this accusation) because they would lock themselves within one ideological perspective or horizon and would recognize only rights supported by or helpful to that perspective.[315] Roberto Unger's experimental project and destabilization rights presents an exception to this comment on the Crits but raises separate difficulties.[316]

C. Point of View Analysis Presented

H. L. A. Hart, as we have noted several times, describes rights as conclusions drawn within a system of rules by way of ruling, claim, or criticism.[317] While the system of rules provides a shared reference point, the official who makes a ruling and the law review editor who writes a criticism may draw different conclusions from the system of rules. Hart is using Point of View analysis when he recognizes the different perspectives from which meaningful statements about rights may be made.[318] A simple form of Point of View analysis may be helpful in the law school classroom. A first year student often will ask what the answer is. The proper reply is that there is no abstract right answer in the sense he is demanding. However, there may be good and cogent arguments for the plaintiff and the defendant and a sound way for a judge to arrive at a decision. Indeed, an attorney counseling a client may perceive the options normally available to a judge in a system of open textured rules and may develop a plan for his client which will guard against the several alternative rulings which a judge may make. There is, then, a planning point of view. The perspectives of attorneys for the plaintiff, defendant and client in need of planning and counseling correspond roughly to Hart's claimant's point of view.[319] The judge's perspective is that of Hart's official.[320] It is worth noting that the answer one gives to a legal question may differ depending upon the role one is playing or the law job one is performing. In discussing or analyzing any statement of law, then, it would be helpful to ask who is making it and what role or law job he is peforming. More generally, in analyzing any statement of law, it would be helpful to recognize the point of view or perspective from which it is made. For example, it could be the ruling of an official, a claim by a litigant, or a criticism by a law review editor.

A social scientist, such as Stuart Scheingold, often is engaged in a descriptive task.[321] It is worth stating the obvious, namely that the craft of the social scientist and the craft of the lawyer are different. Very few of the law jobs just described involve primarily descriptive tasks. Rather, the lawyers performing those jobs are making arguments, plans, or decisions. One engaged, then, in describing the behavior of lawyers, or of a segment of society, or the operation of a legal or political system is performing a task that is different than that of a judge or a litigating attorney. The point of view or perspective of a social scientist is different, then, from that of a judge because the role or task he is performing is different. Some legal philosophers undertake a task that is primarily descriptive. In *The Concept of Law*, H. L. A. Hart offers a number of great clarifying concepts which will help in describing any legal system.[322]

In assessing a descriptive statement it is often helpful to know the purpose of the descriptive statement or what is being described. For example, Stuart Scheingold wants to describe law as part of a larger political system; however, he is describing primarily American law and American politics.[323] While H. L. A. Hart is describing a legal system, or rather offering clarifying concepts which will be helpful in describing a legal system, he is concerned not with the American or British legal systems but with any legal system. When discussing or analyzing any descriptive statement it would be helpful first to recognize that it is a descriptive statement rather than some other use of language such as an argument of law or the decision of a judge. It is also important to ask the purpose of the description and to know what is being described.

Scientists and social scientists traditionally take a descriptive point of view. They are concerned with developing theories or testing hypothesis that offer a more or less adequate representation or description of the world. In contrast, some philosophers, particularly some ethicists, are not concerned with description but rather want to prescribe correct conduct. A number of disciplines have a heavily prescriptive as opposed to a descriptive element. Law perceived from a judge's perspective may be heavily prescriptive. However, a practicing attorney attempting to predict what judges will in fact do may be engaged in a descriptive task. However, when he counsels, or plans for his client, or argues to a court, he may be prescribing rather than describing.

In legal philosophy confusion may arise because different philosophers are speaking from different perspectives. An analytical philosopher such as H. L. A. Hart may set as his task the development of clarifying concepts which will help us in describing and understanding any legal system.[324] An early legal realist such as Llewellyn in his youth may want to offer tools for discovering real rules as opposed to paper rules.[325] These are essentially descriptive rather than prescriptive tasks. However, other philosophers such as the older Llewellyn[326] or Ronald Dworkin[327] may want to improve judicial decision making methods. That is a prescriptive task, and the thinker is taking the perspective of a judge rather than a practicing attorney attempting to predict what the judge will in fact do.

In analyzing any statement on rights, then, it would be

helpful to ask from what point of view or perspective it is made. Is it a ruling, a claim, a prediction, or a criticism? Is it an attempt to describe a legal system or is it a prescription for judges or others? Arguably, regular use of Point of View analysis will resolve a number of apparent head-on conflicts between differing understandings of rights offered by twentieth century legal philosophers. When the point of view from which a statement is made is located and a purpose is attributed to the statement, the core of good sense may appear stripped of implications which are too broad. What a philosopher asserts may be true within a narrow context provided it is not construed as a denial of other understandings of rights. Perhaps all the statements concerning rights discussed earlier in this book contain significant insights and a core of good sense provided the limitations contained in many of the statements on a broader or differing understanding of rights are removed.

D. A Model for Understanding Rights Discourse

Every statement regarding rights is made within a horizon and from a point of view. That is a simple statement of central concepts in the proposed model and provides a powerful set of analytical tools for understanding any statement regarding rights. We will understand a rights statement better if we ask from what point of view it is made, whether it is a descriptive or prescriptive statement, whether it is an argument by plaintiff's or defendant's counsel, whether it is a ruling by a judge and so on; we also will understand it better if we attempt to analyze the horizon of the one making the statement. Nevertheless, a model for understanding rights discourse must be complex and should be set forth more formally. It should begin with a series of assumptions including those concerning horizons and point of view, should include a description of a pluralist society in terms of horizons, and should explain how rights are used in a pluralist society to communicate across horizons, to establish, change, talk about, fight about, reconcile and struggle with human relations. Horizon analysis also may be used to explain some problems for rights discourse in a pluralist society particularly when rights are perceived within one horizon as conclusions drawn within a system of rules.

At least four assumptions provide a foundation for the proposed model:

1. Law is not merely open-textured but often radically open-textured. Karl Llewellyn once described sixty-four orthodox ways of dealing with relevant precedent.[328] Duncan Kennedy has explained the power of recharacterization of law or facts as means for changing the context of the legal argument either in the immediate case or in a series of cases over time.[329] In view of the rise and fall of legal doctrine (liability for negligence without privity of contract, liability in warranty, strict liability in tort,[330] liability under Lemon Laws[331] or Magnuson-Moss)[332] it should be recognized that legal doctrine is subject to radical change through recharacterization as well as other means. Law may be a system of rules but it is a system of radically open-textured rules. If morality is perceived as a system of rules or perhaps several alternate systems of rules, then those rules also may be radically open-textured.

2. Every statement, including every statement regarding rights, is made within a horizon. If a right is a conclusion drawn within a system of radically open-textured rules, then the horizon of the one drawing the conclusion influences the manner in which the conclusion is drawn and the result reached. Horizons create or confine vision and, hence, affect our ability to perceive issues, to recognize

possibilities for recharacterizing law or facts, and to choose between alternate characterizations or competing arguments.

3. Every legal statement including every statement regarding rights is made from a point of view. A person who perceives rights within a horizon nevertheless from time to time may make rights statements from several points of view. Without changing his general horizons he may serve as plaintiff's counsel, defendant's counsel or judge. He may write an article from a descriptive or prescriptive perspective. To understand his rights statement it may be helpful to recognize his point of view as well as to analyze his horizon.

4. Every rights statement is made either from an academic perspective or for one or more of the purposes described in the catalog of the uses of rights.[333] [Academic statements, however, often track uses of rights outside the ivory tower as demonstrated by the catalog of rights which was derived from academic statements.] Typically, rights statements are official rulings such as a decision of a judge, claims or criticism. In the reasoning process of an official or even a private person, rights statements are typically reasons for the conclusion drawn and may trump competing reasons. Often rights statements are made for extraneous reasons in the course of the human struggle. Rights statements, for example, may be made to advance interests or to accumulate resources for the political struggle. When rights statements are made by an official, either as conclusions drawn within a system of rules or as reasons for that conclusion, the official may make the statements without crossing horizons. He also may cross or transcend horizons in the process of arriving at his conclusion. Frequently those who assert rights as claims either in official forums or in the political process are communicating across horizons. Those who claim rights

and the persons who will recognize or accept them often perceive rights within different horizons. When reasons are asserted by the claimants to support their claim of rights those reasons are often, but not always, reasons which would appear respectable in the foreign horizon of those who are asked to recognize or accept the claim. This analysis also applies to long term political campaigns for the advance of interests such as those of a minority group. The campaigners are claimants appealing to those in other horizons as well as their own adherents.

A rights statement may be made to advance a cause within a society which is opposed to that cause. An anti-rights statement also may be made to advance a cause within a moderately hostile society where an impacted version of rights or particular rights acts as an obstacle to the cause. In this sense, anti-rights rhetoric may serve as a peculiar version of rights rhetoric and may be used to hammer on foreign horizons or as a means to encourage one's adherents and to attack one's foes (anti-rights rhetoric as resources). If an ideological cause is successful then rights rhetoric may be used from all points of view and for many of the purposes listed in the catalog of rights for the ultimate purpose of advancing or securing the ideological cause. Anti-rights rhetoric may be used for a similar set of purposes. Here, when an ideological cause is successful, there may be an example of rights or anti-rights rhetoric used within a single horizon with a determined refusal to consider other horizons.

The assumptions just listed are a sufficient basis for rejecting as too simplistic a model in which rights are perceived solely as conclusions drawn within a system of rules, a model which may be equatable with an understanding of rights as entitlements. Rather, the assumptions sketch the beginnings of a model for understanding rights discourse in which the human struggle, the ongoing process of creating, changing, and conversing about relations between persons, has an important role.

To understand rights discourse more fully as part of the human struggle it would be helpful to add to the model an understanding of a pluralist society in terms of horizons. A pluralist society is one in which there are multiple horizons, some of which overlap. Some persons in a pluralist society share horizons as lawyers or economists within their own disciplines to some extent share a common horizon. Nevertheless, different lawyers may perceive radically open-textured legal rules differently because in addition to their shared horizon their perception is affected by horizons which they do not share including moral horizons.

In a pluralist society, then, there are multiple horizons within which legal rules are interpreted. Some horizons contain moral commitments, moral insights, rules or systems of rules as well as political, social and cultural background which affect the interpretation of both legal and moral rules. Often in a pluralist society horizons overlap allowing shared interpretations and understandings between persons of varied horizons. Horizons can be crossed or transcended. Nevertheless, every statement of rights is made from a point of view and within a horizon. Those horizons and points of view are sufficiently different to make it difficult to understand statements of rights without shared horizons, without horizon and point of view analysis, or without an effort to cross or transcend horizons.

A model of rights discourse in a pluralist society, then, would include a recognition that every statement regarding rights is made within a horizon and from a point of view. It would include a recognition that in a complex pluralist society there are multiple horizons and points of view and a recognition that some horizons overlap and that horizons can be crossed or transcended. Horizons, as well as points of view, affect the interpretation given to rights and legal rules and may contain systems of moral rules, moral insights, or moral commitments which interplay with the interpretations of legal rules and statements of rights. Within the context of a pluralistic society as just described, rights statements are made for multiple purposes; rights and rights statements have many uses. Rights statements are made to draw conclusions within systems of legal or moral rules, perhaps as a holding in a judicial decision, or as a reason for a holding. Rights statements are claims, demands, or criticism, they are made for the purpose of promoting interests, attacking opponents or gathering adherents. Almost always rights statements are an attempt to communicate, sometimes passionately, and in a pluralist society often across horizons. In a pluralist society that communication is often difficult. In the history of our pluralist society new rights regularly have been recognized. Despite the difficulties, then, communication through rights discourse across horizons is possible. In some circumstances the assertion of rights is an attempt to call the attention of persons in other horizons to one's interests and oppression. The assertion of rights will be successful only if there are shared horizons, the assertion finds a place in the horizon of others, or others undertake or are persuaded to undertake to transcend or cross horizons in order to understand and recognize those rights.

James Boyd White's understanding of law as rhetoric[334] offers a valuable basis for one interpretation of the model just described. Society in this understanding could be viewed as constituted by the rhetorical discussion concerning what society should be. In a pluralist society, that is one with multiple horizons, individuals and groups are conducting that discussion across horizons in an effort to understand and appeal to arguments and convictions which would appear respectable in the foreign horizon. At the same time, they are seeking recognition of their own positions as perceived within their own horizons. When rights discourse is understood as rhetoric in a society of multiple horizons then that discourse as White perceives may be part of the linkage that constitutes and holds together a diverse pluralist society. If rhetoric is best understood as a sharing of human experience then rights discourse used for the purpose of crossing horizons, of appealing to those in foreign horizons and calling attention to one's own horizon is a method of sharing experience in a complex pluralist society. Horizon analysis offers a more detailed understanding of how that sharing of experience takes place and is an aspect of rights discourse.

E. The Model Applied--Illustrations

(i) The Legal Arena

In *The Concept of Law*,[335] H. L. A. Hart contended that while legal concepts are open-textured, they must have a clear core meaning in order to make communication possible.[336] Lon Fuller, in various replies, always contended that the problems of communication in the core and in the penumbral or open-textured area of legal concepts were not different in kind.[337] Language including legal language, Lon Fuller contended, is always understood in a cultural context or, to use the terms of this book, within a horizon.[338] The core meaning of the same legal concept will be understood differently in various societies and cultures. Lon Fuller's contention may be similar to the position of the Crits that legal language is radically open-textured.[339] If legal language has a clear core meaning in any particular pluralist society, it is because judges and lawyers to some extent share a common horizon within which the language is perceived as having such a core meaning or because the differing horizons of relevant persons such as judges and lawyers overlap sufficiently to allow them to perceive a clear core meaning to a disputed or contested concept.

In *Law's Empire*, under a new and different analysis Ronald Dworkin now supports Lon Fuller's position that there is no difference between our understanding of the core and penumbral areas of legal concepts.[340] All legal conclusions result from an interpretation. Conclusions as to the core meaning of a legal concept may flow more easily but result and should result from the same interpretation used to support conclusions in hard or penumbral cases.[341] Using the analysis in this book the interpretation is made within a horizon and itself may establish a new, perhaps narrow and rigid, horizon. The clear meaning (the core) of legal concepts may result from shared or overlapping horizons within a society.

H. L. A. Hart invented a statute or a village ordinance prohibiting vehicles in the park to illustrate his contention that legal language is open-textured.[342] That statute became an illustration of Lon Fuller's contention that the problems of communication in the core and the penumbra are not different.[343] We can use the statute, here, to illustrate the manner in which legal statements including statements concerning rights are always made within a horizon and from a point of view.

Hart explained that while the statute clearly prohibited motor vehicles there would be a question as to whether it prohibited bicycles, roller skates or baby carriages.[344] These instances would present cases in the penumbral or open-textured area of the statute. Automobiles, on the other hand, would be plainly prohibited by the core meaning of the word "vehicles."[345] Fuller imagined a war memorial, a jeep, which veterans of the Korean War wanted to place in the park and argued that while it was an automobile its presence in the park would not violate the statute.[346] A better example would be a police car or an ambulance racing across the park grass to stop a crime or to rescue the victim of a heart attack. Fuller argued that the word "vehicles" in the statute should be understood in the context of the remaining statutory language particularly the word "park."[347] What vehicles would be prohibited in the park would depend upon the use of parks in the particular society. One could attribute to the legislature or the village council an intention to protect the normal recreational uses of the park; those uses would differ from society to society. A police car attempting to prevent a crime would be protecting rather than interfering with those normal recreational uses and hence would not be prohibited by the statute. As Fuller argued, the problems of interpretation in the core are not different from those in the penumbra.

To illustrate the manner in which statements regarding rights are made within a horizon and from a point of view, it would be helpful to imagine additional circumstances around the enactment and enforcement of a statute prohibiting vehicles in the park. Assume that until recently the park was used primarily by elderly persons who enjoyed sitting in the shade to enjoy the open air and by parents with children twelve years of age and younger. The ordinance was occasioned by a recent invasion of the park by older teenagers with mopeds and motorcycles. In those circumstances, there is a strong argument that bicycles used by younger children, roller skates, and baby carriages are not vehicles prohibited by the statute. Suppose, however, that the older teenagers return to the park with skateboards and engage among other activities in races and other contests. Suppose in addition that the park lies on the border between an ordinary middle-class neighborhood and an area recently occupied by a minority group. Assume that the older teenagers are members of the minority group. In these circumstances the proper recreational uses of the park could be understood differently depending upon one's cultural horizon.

In the legal disputes which could ensue, statements regarding rights could be made from a series of different perspectives or points of view. One point of view would be that of the prosecuting attorney who might contend that the teenagers were violating the rights of the elderly citizens to peaceful enjoyment of the park. That contention would be made from a point of view, that of a litigating attorney charged with prosecuting the teenagers for using skateboards in the park. The statement also would be made within a horizon, possibly that of a middle-class citizen who understands the recreational use of the park by the elderly and is outraged by the teenagers who have disturbed that use. A second point of view would be that of the defense attorney who might contend that the teenagers, too, have a right to reasonable recreational use of the park. Conceivably, the defense attorney shares the horizon of the minority culture and is deeply troubled by the lack of understanding of that culture and the needs of its members. His arguments concerning rights are made both from a point of view, that of defense counsel, and within a horizon, that of the minority culture. The judge, as explained above, has yet a third point of view and a horizon, possibly like the prosecutor that of the middle class but not inconceivably that of the minority culture. The judge's conclusions concerning rights to usage of the park will be conclusions drawn within a system of open-textured rules from a point of view and within a horizon.

In more complex cases, non-legal systems of rules in the judge's horizon may be relevant to the decision. For example, the judge's moral perspective may or may not be perceived by him as embodied in a system of rules. That moral perspective may become relevant to a legal decision perhaps in the manner described by Ronald Dworkin.[348] Where several parties to a case have differing moral horizons, multiple sets of moral rules may be relevant in understanding the dispute.

Passion or desire also may be relevant to understanding or deciding the dispute. As described above, the prosecuting attorney may be outraged at the violation of the rights of the elderly to recreational use of the park. The judge may share that outrage. In contrast, the members of the minority culture may be outraged at their oppression which they perceive as represented by the efforts to keep them out of the park. A statement of rights may be a passionate objection to an invasion of deep interests. It may be an effort to call attention to one's circumstances, to one's personality, or to one's oppression. When made as part of a law reform campaign or by a judge committed to change, a statement of rights may be a demand for new arrangements in society, for a new pattern of human relationships. Even in a simple dispute such as that over the use of the park there may be a demand for a new pattern of human relationships which is represented by a statement regarding rights.

Those claiming rights particularly but not exclusively as yet unrecognized rights have a large task of persuasion. The claimants may perceive rights within a cultural, political, or moral horizon not shared by the majority or dominant culture. Their claim of right may represent a statement of oppression passionately felt by them but not perceived by the dominant classes in society. The claim of right becomes a means for communicating their oppression and desire for change. It is a means for communicating insights from their horizon to those who perceive the relevant issues and rules within other horizons. Nevertheless, the claim of right will be recognized only to the extent that it finds a place in the horizons of the dominant classes or to the extent that members of the dominant classes are persuaded to cross or transcend horizons.

In a pluralistic society, one with multiple horizons within each of which radically open-textured legal rules are differently interpreted, claims of right become a means for communicating across horizons, for calling attention to oppression, and potentially for reconciling human relations. A danger is that critical actors in the human struggle, including judges, may perceive rights only within their own narrowly defined horizons and will attempt neither to cross nor transcend horizons. It is helpful in understanding the relation between law and the human struggle to recognize the phenomenon of horizons. In understanding the conflicting statements of rights in that human struggle it would be helpful to recognize that every statement regarding rights is made within a horizon and from a point of view and for one of the purposes set forth in the catalog of rights.[349]

Dworkin's insistence in *Law's Empire* on integrity as a virtue of law itself may serve as an illustration of rights perceived within a narrow, rigid horizon.[350] Judge Hercules, Dworkin's imaginary judge, should develop an interpretation of law itself as well as of the Constitution and legal principles.[351] To promote friendship in society, Judge

Hercules should maintain rigorous consistency in his decisions, a consistency made possible by adhering in his decisions to his interpretation of law itself. In his remarks on friendship, Dworkin explains that while one may disagree with a friend, one expects consistency or rather the integrity of consistency from one's friend even in areas where one believes he is wrong.[352] If one could imagine the law personified as a friend one would ask integrity of it, the integrity of consistency even when wrong. Hercules, then, will be confined in his decision making by a narrow horizon established by his interpretation of law, itself arrived at within a horizon. Hercules adhering to the virtue of integrity will refuse to move beyond the narrow horizon established by his interpretation. In comment, I suppose I would expect of my friend that he would listen to me and would be open to understanding and perhaps responding to what I have to say. The virtue of a listening openness has been a traditional virtue of the common law judge and one we could expect of the law if we were to personify it as a friend. A commitment to crossing horizons, then, is an important commitment for an ideal judge in a pluralist society.

The Crits, despite their emphasis on deconstruction, also illustrate the danger that important actors in the human struggle may perceive rights only within their own narrowly defined horizons, here the horizons established by their own particular political ideologies. See, for example, how Duncan Kennedy imagining himself as a judge in "Freedom and Constraint in Adjudication: A Critical Phenomenology" describes the imaginary case before him in a manner designed to promote his ideological position.[353] The Crits may use rights rhetoric or anti-rights rhetoric to advance their ideological causes. That may be an appropriate use of rights or anti-rights discourse as advocates in a pluralist society. From that point of view, it is a means of hammering on foreign horizons. From the point of view of a judge, however, referring conclusions, analysis, and rights or anti-rights rhetoric to an ideology is a way of refusing to cross horizons, of refusing to listen to those in foreign horizons.

James Boyd White's understanding of law as rhetoric, on the other hand, appears compatible with horizon crossing from multiple different points of view, including that of the judge.[354] Rhetoric, as the exchange of experiences, and as the argument about what society should be which constitutes society would seem groundable in Dworkin's understanding of friendship as Dworkin's own understanding of integrity is not. One who exchanges experiences is one who listens to another as a friend.

(ii) The Academic World

When analyzing academic statements regarding rights, perhaps point of view analysis would be more helpful than is generally recognized. We are familiar with the need to understand philosophers, including legal philosophers, in view of the problems or the questions normally asked in, and the general atmosphere of their age of the world. Legal philosophers regularly have philosophical horizons, created by the influence of non-legal philosophical thought. Llewellyn, for example, was influenced by American Pragmatism. It is worth recognizing, however, that he taught Commercial Law, was the chief reporter for the Uniform Commercial Code and probably viewed law from the point of view of a practicing attorney attempting to predict what courts will in fact do. By the time he wrote the *Common Law Tradition*,[355] he probably had shifted his point of view to the perspective of the lawmaker, the legislator or the judge. To understand his statements concerning rights, it would be helpful to recognize his point of view as well as his philosophical and law reform horizons. Recognizing the various philosophical horizons within which academic statements about rights are made, we may remain content to let disputing theorists pass each other in the night. Point of view analysis may prevent that. By recognizing the point of view from which seemingly inconsistent statements are made, we may be able to extract the good sense from each, reconcile the conflicting positions and further the grand conversation. Point of view analysis, then, may become a means for crossing horizons.

In applying point of view analysis to academic statements regarding rights, it may be helpful to classify some as descriptive and others as prescriptive. Hart,[356] Llewellyn[357] and Scheingold[358] have made statements about rights from a descriptive perspective. Dworkin[359] and the pragmatic instrumentalists discuss rights from a prescriptive perspective. The Crits, Feminists, and Outsiders would normally seem to be adopting the prescriptive point of view of an advocate.[360] White's understanding of law as rhetoric would appear to be an attempt not only to describe but prescribe.[361] Some efforts in deconstructing rights and other legal doctrine have made significant contributions to our descriptive understanding of law, to the understanding of law for example as radically open-textured.

(a) Descriptive Points of View

When analyzing statements about rights made from a descriptive perspective, it is helpful to ask what is described and the purpose of the description. For example, sometimes a descriptive statement is made from the point of view of a practicing attorney attempting to predict what a court will in fact do, and sometimes from the point of view of a social scientist attempting to describe the role of law within a political system.

H. L. A. Hart is a philosopher concerned with language

and system who, in *The Concept of Law*, offers great clarifying concepts that will be helpful in describing any legal system.[362] His perspective is descriptive and he is concerned ultimately with the description of legal systems. Both in *The Concept of Law*[363] and in "Definition and Theory in Jurisprudence"[364] he is concerned also with describing and clarifying language usage.

In contrast, while Llewellyn often makes statements about law and rights from a descriptive perspective, he is concerned with describing law in action and human behavior[365] as opposed to rules or language usage. Often adopting the perspective of a practicing attorney attempting to predict what courts will in fact do, he wants to describe the behavior of judges and to develop or critique the tools for predicting that behavior.[366]

From that perspective, it is appealing and perhaps accurate to state that there is no right without a remedy. A practicing attorney advising a client must be concerned with what courts in fact will do and would be mistaken if he misunderstood his perspective, for example, by thinking of himself as a judge. Arguably, insistence on a predictive perspective provided a significant breakthrough that allowed us to set aside doctrinal analysis and concentrate on the human behavior of judges and others associated with the legal system.[367] The vast array of impact studies[368] by social scientists are legitimate descendants of the realist insistence on a predictive perspective. Again, those concerned with law reform may benefit from concentration on changing what courts in fact will do. The perspective that Llewellyn and others following Holmes offered to law is responsible for significant insights and improved our understanding of law and its practice.[369]

However, Llewellyn overlooked a number of important usages of legal language and offered a distorted understanding of law. Hart properly corrected his analysis in "Definition and Theory in Jurisprudence" and was able to do so because he was concerned with describing language usage rather than predicting the behavior of judges. Nevertheless, Hart, in his published works, is apparently blind to human behavior, aside from that important mode of human behavior, language usage.[370]

Lawyers and legal philosophers often forget that law is a segment of a larger political system. Scheingold, concerned with describing law as part of the American political system, offers a broader understanding of behavior and human relations.[371]

Llewellyn, Hart and Scheingold all offer valuable understandings of law and legal behavior. Their respective analysis of rights are not in conflict when we understand the perspective from which their statements are made. Within the descriptive perspective it is important to ask what is described and the purpose of the description. Llewellyn, Hart and Scheingold described different aspects of law and legal behavior. A more comprehensive understanding of rights must include the contributions of each. Human behavior (including the behavior of judges) concerning rights, the use of the language of rights by those performing various roles in the legal system, and the role of legal behavior regarding rights in the larger political system, are all worth discussing and analyzing.

(b) Prescriptive Points of View

Whatever their other differences, Dworkin, in *Taking Rights Seriously*,[372] and Hart, in *The Concept of Law*,[373] are not in conflict; it is a mistake to believe that they are. In "Hard Cases," Chapter IV of *Taking Rights Seriously*, Dworkin is prescribing a method for deciding cases.[374] When offering that method he takes the point of view of a judge. Hart, in *The Concept of Law* as already noted, takes a descriptive rather than a prescriptive point of view.

Dworkin, however, is influenced by Hart. Like Hart, he understands law as language and system. One could understand Dworkin's judicial method as an example of Hart's descriptive statement that rights are conclusions drawn with a system of rules; Dworkin offers a method for drawing such conclusions. One important aspect of Dworkin's method in *Taking Rights Seriously*, the notion of contested moral concepts, closely resembles Hart's open texture of law: a contested moral concept is an open textured moral concept normally found in constitutional law.[375]

In offering his judicial method, Dworkin insists that his judge relate law which he understands in *Taking Rights Seriously* as an open textured system of rules to one important aspect of life outside that system of rules, namely, morality or the judge's own theory of justice.[376] Hart, in his rare moments of prescription, probably would disagree with this requirement for judicial method.[377] However, Hart's description of law as open textured[378] and of judges as deputy legislators[379] who make law within that open texture does not preclude Dworkin's prescription for a judicial method. One describing law would be inaccurate if he asserted that judges in hard cases governed by open textured concepts or rules do not refer to their own theories of justice in drawing conclusions concerning rights. Hart's clarifying descriptive concept, the open texture of law, accommodates a variety of judicial methods for deciding hard cases presented within that open texture.

In *Law's Empire*, Dworkin challenges Hart's description of law as open-textured with different modes of decision making within the core and penumbral areas.[380] He argues that Hart, along with others, offers a theory, which Dworkin calls the semantic sting, which is mistakenly characterized as a theory about language, that is, a semantic theory.[381] Dworkin argues that Hart's analysis of law as open-textured is best understood as an interpretation of law or as a post-interpretative theory which he labels and discusses as Conventionalism.[382] Dworkin prefers his own theory of law as Integrity[383] to the interpretation, very like Hart's which he refers to as Conventionalism. Law as Integrity is a prescriptive understanding of judicial method erected on a descriptive understanding of law as interpretation and rejection of Hart's and Dworkin's earlier descriptive understanding of law as open-textured.

One large conglomeration of thinkers who would disagree with Dworkin's prescription for judicial decision making method would be those whom Summers describes as pragmatic instrumentalists.[384] Holmes, who is an intellectual ancestor of the pragmatic instrumentalists, undertook to prescribe as well as describe. In the "Path of the Law",[385] he offered his famous descriptive understanding of law from the point of view of a practicing attorney when he stated that law was the predictions of what judges will in fact do.[386] Later in the same speech, however, he shifts from the point of view of the practicing attorney to that of the judge and states:

> I think that the judges themselves have failed adequately to recognize their duty of weighing considerations of social advantage. The duty is inevitable, and the result of the often proclaimed judicial aversion to deal with such considerations is simply to leave the very ground and foundation of judgments inarticulate, and often unconscious.....[387]

Holmes, in this statement, offers from a prescriptive perspective the beginnings of a judicial method. His method contains an important prescription -- be concerned with "considerations of social advantage".[388] The pragmatic instrumentalists following Holmes were concerned with social advantages and as Summers suggests, would consider rights as social goals or as means for achieving social goals.[389]

However, some of those whom Summers describes as pragmatic instrumentalists, namely the early legal realists, often were concerned with description rather than prescription.[390] Indeed, an important way of distinguishing legal realists from sociological jurisprudence, both of whom Summers describes as pragmatic instrumentalists,[391] is to note that the legal realists were often concerned with description usually from the point of view of a practicing attorney while sociological jurisprudence usually prescribed, often for judges.[392]

When prescribing for judges the legal realists like sociological jurisprudence were concerned with considerations of social advantage.[393] However, there were important carry-overs from their descriptive understanding of law which may have been overlooked in sociological jurisprudence. Taking seriously, from the point of view of the practicing attorney Holmes' description of law as predictions of what judges will do, the legal realists found that it was difficult to make accurate predictions with the then extant tools for doing so. Ultimately, the reason for this difficulty was that judges are human with human failings, inclinations and perceptions.[394] It may be that attempting to predict what judges will in fact do is an important key opening the door to an understanding of the human dimensions of law. The legal realists in their prescriptive mode retained the insights developed from this breakthrough on the descriptive side.[395] Jerome Frank's descriptive and prescriptive understanding of law as three dimensional with a judge or decision maker, a language or rule element and a situation[396] is a result of this breakthrough. A resulting prescription is that a judge should not concern himself solely with flat law, the language or rule element but also should know himself and the factors that might influence his perception or understanding of the situation before him.[397] Llewellyn's judicial method contains elements such as hunching[398] and situation sense [399] which show a similar consciousness of the human dimension of a judge's perception of law and its application to a problem.[400] Both the legal realists and sociological jurisprudence were concerned with social advantage, but unlike sociological jurisprudence, the legal realists brought an understanding of the judge and the factors affecting his perception to their prescriptive contributions to judicial methodology.

Dworkin, despite his emphasis on principles, by and large accepts Hart's descriptive understanding of law as a system of rules. Like Hart, he is concerned with language and system. Principles and ultimately interpretation are ways of understanding language and system. Because Hart's description which Dworkin ultimately accepts in *Taking Rights Seriously* overlooks human behavior, Dworkin's judicial method fails to account for the judge's human failings, inclinations and perceptions.[401] His method is largely directed towards language and rules, what Jerome Frank would call flat law.[402] Again, because Hart's descriptive understanding of law is directed towards systems of rules and not towards law as part of a larger political system, Dworkin's judicial methodology overlooks the relation between law and considerations of social advantage.[403]

Dworkin, in his judicial methodology, adds one aspect of life, namely moral theory, to his understanding of law as language and rules.[304] Pragmatic instrumentalists, while not particularly concerned with moral theory, were concerned with society, societal advantage, and at times with the human beings who participate in a legal system. Summers is correct when he states that moral theory can be incorporated in the pragmatic instrumentalist method and can provide a means for choosing between conflicting social goals.[405] An understanding of rights as trumps and rights as reasons is not incompatible with a view of rights as goals. Dworkin's methodology has made important contributions to improving judicial reasoning.[406] However, Dworkin's insistence that judicial decisions be supported solely by reasons of principle rather than reasons of policy is at odds with the pragmatic instrumentalist emphasis upon considerations of social advantage. Again, that difference may be due to Dworkin's acceptance of a narrow description of law as a system of rules. In *Law's Empire* Dworkin continues to regard law as a system of rules and principles which will be the subject of Hercules' interpretive theory.

Dworkin's rejection in *Law's Empire* of Pragmatism as an interpretative and post-interpretative theory of law[407] if it had been written later could have been directed at Judge Posner's "Pragmatist Manifesto."[408] Both Dworkin's prescriptive understanding of law as Integrity and Posner's defense of Pragmatism are written largely from the point of view of the judge or one advising a judge as to judicial method. Both understandings of law are in fundamental opposition. For example, Dworkin insists that Judge Hercules have an overarching theory[409] while Posner rejects overarching theories.[410] Dworkin insists upon rigorous protection of ordinary legal rights justified by Hercules' interpretation as well as strong constitutional rights.[411] Posner would use ordinary legal reasoning in the normal run of cases to arrive at routine conclusions regarding legal rights but would find no fundamental justification for those conclusions.[412]

Point of view analysis can clarify discussions of law and rights. It can offer a classification of points of view from which statements about rights have been made. But, of course, it cannot resolve all conflicts. Some conflicts are due to deeply held differences concerning judicial method, the function of law, or moral theory. A model for understanding rights discourse should recognize not only that statements regarding rights are made from a point of view and for a purpose such as one of those listed in the catalog of rights but that such statements are made within one or several of the multiple horizons in a pluralistic society.

Point of view analysis is helpful in demonstrating the need for a more complex model for understanding rights discourse. Each of the understandings of rights derived from academic analysis[413] and presented in the catalog of rights[414] offers a too simplistic model of rights which misses important insights concerning rights discourse perceivable from other points of view.

Arguably, the Crits, who have recognized the radical open texture of law and the phenomenon described in this book as horizons, also offer too simplistic an understanding of rights.

Chapter IV

A Higher Interpretation

A. Introduction

The last chapter presented a model for understanding rights discourse in which the hard reference point is the behavior of human beings in talking about, fighting about, establishing, changing and reconciling human relations. Rights discourse is employed for a variety of purposes (see the catalog of the uses of rights) in the course of such behavior. In a pluralist society (one with multiple horizons) with a system of radically open-textured legal rules, rights discourse is a means for communicating across horizons; for example, it is a means of calling attention to oppression. In contrast, rights discourse is also a means for refusing to cross horizons; a judge may understand legal rules within his own horizon and recognize rights as conclusions drawn within that system of rules without crossing horizons. The model presented allows us to analyze and understand rights discourse in relation to human behavior, to the human struggle.

In this chapter, a higher interpretation of rights discourse and the model will be offered. Ultimately, the higher interpretation will make it possible to recognize a different hard reference point for understanding rights and a different set of strategies for dealing with rights discourse as part of the human struggle. From the perspective afforded by recognizing commitments such as advancing the cause of humanity, affording all persons deep respect and concern, or simply promoting the stability of society, an additional use of rights discourse may be perceived, namely as a means for conducting conversations concerning human relations between persons with different horizons who perceive rights and relations differently. The hard reference point is the sense of obligation grounded in the same or similar human commitments. Rights and the language of rights are used within and across horizons to appeal to obligations which others recognize or which it is claimed they should recognize. A judge (or other official) grounds his conclusions as to the rights of litigants in his perception of his obligations. His decision to transcend or cross horizons while struggling to reach conclusions also would be grounded in his sense of obligation.

The following discussion will begin with a description of conversation as a use of rights discourse,[415] followed by an analysis of conversation in relation to fundamental human commitments,[416] and will conclude with an elucidation of rights as grounded in obligations.[417]

The conclusions presented in this chapter should be recognized as post interpretative, that is they are reached on the basis of certain assumptions as to human goals and aspirations. If one accepts a commitment to humanity, to affording all persons deep respect and concern, to the stability of society or the like, then one may perceive rights as grounded in obligation; after discussion one may be persuaded to accept an obligation to cross or transcend horizons in order to converse with those of different views. One should note that the various human goals and aspirations which would support this higher interpretation of rights discourse are shared at least partially by many participants in the grand conversation.

B. Conversation, Its Possibility

The possibility of conversation across horizons and some of the means for conducting such a conversation are illustrated by the grand conversation between twentieth century legal philosophers. H. L. A. Hart, the host of the salon for that grand conversation, can serve as a role model. While Dworkin, Rawls and other recent thinkers have developed theories which may enhance conversation, Hart has practiced the art by conducting conversations with many of the leading philosophers of law.[418] One aspect of the art as practiced by Hart is to accept insights developed by other thinkers, rescue those insights from the competing view of legal philosophy and transform them so that those insights can become part of Hart's understanding of law. Very probably Hart's concept, the open-texture of law,[419] was derived from legal realism and most particularly from Llewellyn's notion of leeways in the law[420] which it closely resembles and generalizes. A second example is Hart's rule of recognition[421] which is a transformation of Hans Kelsen's concept, grundnorm.[422]

In a like manner, a judge who holds a deep position while engaged in conversation with a fellow judge, may recognize an important insight, may accept that insight, relate it to his own deep position and then perceive an obligation to recognize a concrete right which he would not have perceived otherwise. The two positions may then converge to produce a holding establishing that concrete right. If both judges are using horizon-crossing techniques and are committed to crossing horizons, the possibility will be enhanced that, in the course of conversation, each judge will recognize opportunities for convergence which are consistent with each judge's perceptions of his own obligations.

Ronald Dworkin's method for judicial decision making in *Taking Rights Seriously* and perhaps in *Law's Empire* offers an opportunity to describe more precisely how such a conversation between judges with different horizons could be conducted. Dworkin's method requires a judge to develop a conceptualization, a theory or understanding for each of the great contested moral concepts in the United States Constitution.[423] The judge's conceptualization or theory should explain the concept and the clear instances to which the concept applies as well as provide a basis for the decision the judge wants to reach in a particular case and for his decisions in future cases.[424] One could imagine a Supreme Court composed of nine judges with differing moral and political horizons who, nevertheless, are committed to Dworkin's methodology for judicial decision making. While each judge must offer a theory of relevant constitutional concepts, his theory will overlap and converge with those of his fellows to the extent that each would explain the same contested concept and would support the same result in clear instances. While each judge's theory might support differing conclusions in hard or penumbral cases, it is also possible that differing theories would converge in support of the same decision in some of those cases. Since each judge is explaining the same contested concepts, it is possible that one judge will recognize the brilliance of another judge's analysis and will seek to incorporate his fellow's insights in his own explanation. Using Dworkin's method, he would do so by relating those insights to his own deep theory and to the contested concept and the agreed upon instances of the contested concept.[425] A similar method for conversation and for ruling under great contested concepts may follow from a judge's acceptance of Dworkin's prescriptions in *Law's Empire*.[426] An interpretation of law, of our government and our constitution will overlap with other interpretations of the same phenomenon in the same age of society and will make conversation and convergence possible and at times likely particularly if judges with different interpretations share other horizons such as political liberalism.

Using Dworkin's method to describe an imagined conversation between Supreme Court judges brings out an important aspect of a judge's work. In their written opinions and during conference, judges who hold differing deep positions would be regularly engaged in offering rational justifications for their decisions. In other words, the justices would be engaged in regular rational argument and conversation which sometimes would produce agreement.[427] Since appointments to the United States Supreme Court are the result of a political process, one can imagine a number of deep positions rotating on the Court allowing a number of subcultures and their deeply held views of life and law to be represented from time to time on the Court. The Court, then, would be a device for engaging various deep views on our society in regular rational argument and conversation which sometimes would result in convergence.

Pragmatic Instrumentalist method, when related to deep theories in the choice of goals, would offer the opportunity for similar rational argument and conversation. Summers, in his critical examination of pragmatic instrumentalist value theory, suggests that fundamental theories of government or justice such as those contemplated by Dworkin could serve as a basis for choosing between goals.[428] The goals so chosen then could provide a foundation for means-goal reasoning and the decision of cases according to pragmatic-instrumentalist method. It is possible then that some pragmatic instrumentalist judges could agree with

Dworkin on the role of theory while disagreeing with him on decision making method. A pragmatic instrumentalist judge may recognize an important societal goal such as the pursuit of truth through robust discussion in a democratic society. His acceptance of that societal goal may be grounded in a desire to advance the cause of humanity or a commitment to afford each person in his pursuit of truth, deep respect and concern. The obligation to support the societal goal of the pursuit of truth through robust discussion would be grounded in his deep commitments and, in turn, would support an obligation to take seriously the rights of freedom of speech and the press. Judges using the method just described could converse and converge in rational argument in the same manner as judges who follow Dworkin's method more rigorously. Dworkin's Judge Hercules, despite his more rigid approach, could join in that conversation and converge with the conclusions of the more pragmatic judges.

One should recognize that a characteristic of pragmatic instrumentalist judges was openness to new ideas, new values, new demands. Some pragmatic instrumentalists such as Pound and Llewellyn developed devices which could be described as means for crossing horizons. A concern for impact and interest analysis, for the location and balancing of relevant interests in view of the impact of proposed rules upon them, is a means for understanding the human needs of others who may not share the decision maker's horizons.[429] Llewellyn's notion of situation sense requires the judge in a disciplined manner to penetrate the horizons of litigants to understand the context of the dispute before applying legal rules in its resolution.[430] A judge whose decision making method requires the regular use of situation sense is committed by his methodology to cross horizons before deciding cases. Arguably, crossing horizons through the use of such methods as impact and interest analysis and situation sense is necessary in order to take human beings and their claims of right seriously. Judge Hercules,[431] following Dworkin's method, may be a classic example of a judge who rigorously draws conclusions within a system of rules perceived within one horizon, the horizon established by his deep theory and strongly defended against outside influence, including cries of oppression, by the methodological demand for consistency.

Some Critical Legal Studies theory may be described as offering a mirror image or a photographic negative of Dworkin's methodology. With Dworkin, they recognize the importance of deep theory or interpretation of law which they would describe as ideological commitment. While aware of the manner in which ideological commitment either accepted by the individual or inherited with one's culture from the past creates horizons, they use that understanding as a basis for criticism rather than to create horizon crossing methods in their own decision making process. Rather, one would suspect that like Dworkin's Judge Hercules, a Crit judge would endeavor, as long as politically expedient, to make his decisions rigorously consistent with his deep theory, his ideology. He might explain that all judicial decision making is political and that the best means for advancing the cause of humanity is to promote the movement. Query whether the probable resulting failure to recognize cries of oppression from foreign horizons promotes the cause of humanity.

The Legal Realists whom the Crits claim as intellectual ancestors and whom Summers classifies as Pragmatic Instrumentalists probably did not develop horizon crossing techniques such as situation sense until they had changed point of view from the perspective of the practicing attorney attempting to predict what courts will in fact do to the perspective of the lawmaker. One could describe two modes in the Legal Realist understanding of law, an earlier critical mode in which they recognized the open texture of law and the multiple influences on a judge's decision making process and a later creative mode in which they developed methods for decision making, including situation sense, adjusted to and acknowledging the aspects of law originally perceived in the critical mode. One can detect an early beginning of a change in Critical Legal Studies thought from a critical to a creative mode in the writings of Roberto Unger and Duncan Kennedy. For example, Kennedy's article, "Freedom and Constraint in Adjudication: A Critical Phenomenology,"[432] offers an analysis of a decision making process which he might employ in the role of a United States District Court Judge. Part of the analysis is a dialogue between "How I Want to Come Out" (HIWTCO) and the case law.[433] He concedes that the dialogue with the wisdom of other judges might alter HIWTCO and result in a different holding than he would imagine at the beginning of the dialogue.[434] Kennedy presents an example of conversation with horizon crossing possibilities despite the political orientation of a Critical Legal Studies judge. While recognizing that this is an early example of a possible creative mode in Crit thought, one also should note the limitations on Kennedy's willingness to cross horizons. His dialogue, for example, like the conversation and rational argument of a judge employing Dworkin's method, is entirely on the doctrinal level. He does not employ Pragmatic Instrumentalist horizon crossing techniques such as impact and interest analysis or situation sense which are concerned with discovering the problems of people rather than the discussion of doctrine.

Judge Posner in contrast insists upon rejecting

overarching theories although he undoubtedly has an interpretation of law implicit in his entire approach, at a minimum the interpretation described by Dworkin in *Law's Empire* as Pragmatism.[435] Posner undoubtedly is constrained by other aspects of his horizons in his understanding and interpretation of the task of judicial decision making. See for example his now subordinated commitment to wealth maximization.[436] Nevertheless, his lack of an explicitly articulated overarching theory leaves him free to roam, to explore, to engage in conversation and to absorb insights. See, for example, his conversations with Robin West from which he has accepted insights now incorporated in his view of law.[437] His use of ordinary legal reasoning probably contains horizon crossing devices although unlike other pragmatic instrumentalists he does not deliberately develop and incorporate such devices in his decision making method. Nevertheless, his use of social science method[438] will assist in crossing horizons as will his abandonment of a rigid insistence on wealth maximization as primary. The lack of an articulated interpretation of law, however, may hinder exchange of views and conversations between deep positions. Nevertheless, his strong representation of the Law and Economics school[439] may substitute for an articulated overarching theory.

Ultimately, of course, James Boyd White offers an understanding of law and society in which legal argumentation is ideally and often actually conversation, a conversation which can be an exchange of human experience, and which constitutes society as a relationship between persons engaged in argument over what society should be.[440] Rights rhetoric is part of that conversation and a means of crossing horizons and carrying forward that argument and holding together a pluralist society composed of multiple horizons.[441] West has suggested the alternate use of narrative and rights rhetoric.[442] Narrative is an alternate form of discourse which would allow us to share experiences across horizons.

Despite the genuine obstacles, then, a conversation across horizons is possible and twentieth century legal philosophers have developed techniques for conducting it. Some techniques enhance dialogue on the intellectual and doctrinal level. Others are designed for discerning the impact of legal doctrine on the persons affected by law and for understanding in the process of legal decision making the relevant non-legal horizons. Some such as those offered by White and West are means for sharing experiences across horizons.

C. Why Converse?

Dworkin accepts a commitment to afford all persons deep respect and concern.[443] In *Law's Empire,* he argues for consistency in law on the basis of a commitment to friendship in society.[444] H. L. A. Hart, as a utilitarian in morals, has a commitment to humanity which he shares with many pragmatic instrumentalists. Some Crits are committed to the cause of humanity, to human interconnectedness and community, or to civic virtue. Commitments which would support a desire for conversation may appear in a variety of shapes and dimensions. A shallow commitment shared by a number of social scientists as well as others is a commitment to stability in society.[445]

One would be concerned with the ideas and insights intellectually grounded in commitments which one does not share or developed in foreign horizons not merely because of curiosity or fascination with all things human but because one respects the intellectual integrity and development of one's fellow human beings. Reciprocal relations which would be desired for similar reasons between those engaged in governance or with the governed would be promoted by conversation and the crossing of horizons.

Rights, reciprocal relations and conversation across horizons are connected concepts and phenomenon which are worth exploring. It may not be meaningful to talk of rights in the absence of relationships between persons. An atheist on a desert island alone in the world after an atomic war has neither rights nor obligations. But it is meaningful to talk of rights as a means for establishing and carrying forward relations. The distribution of tasks and rewards in a small group may arise from implicitly established reciprocal relations. For example, it may be arranged, perhaps by customary action, that the task of washing the supper dishes rotates each evening among the members of a small group living together. It may be established also that leftover dessert such as the extra piece of pie belongs to the person who does the dishes. The group, then, may be said to have a right to have a particular person do the dishes on a certain day. Likewise, that person has a right to the extra piece of pie. While the rights originally developed from the customary reciprocal relations, explicit recognition of the rights perhaps following a dispute will affect subsequent behavior. On the rule level, the person whose turn it is has a duty to do the dishes and the group has a duty to leave the extra piece of pie for him.

In a society governed in part by a legal system, a minority may claim certain rights through litigation or otherwise. That claim could be described as an attempt to gain recognition, to say - here we are, we are citizens too - and to establish relationships with society. Recognition of the right by a court may produce actual behavior in society including the establishment of new relationships. Following

Brown v. Board of Education,[446] for example, children attended new schools, had new teachers and hence new relationships. Scheingold would describe the success of *Brown* as an expansion of the myth of rights.[447] Using the analysis in this book, many in society slowly recognized not merely a legal duty but a deep obligation to accept the rights established by the Supreme Court in *Brown*. Recognition of rights and the correlated obligations or duties are significant ways of establishing relationships in small groups and in society.

One important use of rights and correlated obligations in a pluralist society is to relate significant groups or deep views of life and law to each other. The politics of rights as described by Scheingold,[448] the constitutional litigation process and Supreme Court decision making as described earlier[449] are important means for changing, developing and carrying forward the relationship between groups and deep views in our society. The ability to use these processes and the conversation, sometimes rational, which arises from their use helps to establish reciprocal[450] relations in society even if the campaign or litigation is not successful. At least there was a chance to campaign, to litigate and to be heard while offering rational argument. By performing these actions the group has participated in society and is prepared to allow competing groups to do the same. Conversation, itself, is a relationship in which exchange takes place. Conversation on a grand scale about rights is one of the means by which relationships are established and stability is promoted in our society.

The conversation which promotes reciprocal relations may be desired because one is concerned for humanity, has deep respect and concern for each of one's fellows, or simply because one desires the stability in society which would be promoted by conversation and reciprocal relations. Beyond the desire for intellectual exchange and reciprocal relations promoted by conversation, one may desire to learn through crossing horizons and conversation about the impact of legal rules and societal structures on humanity, on portions of it, or on persons for whom one has deep respect and concern. Before one makes a legal rule or creates a societal structure, perhaps in response to a deep commitment or an ideological goal, one may want to assess its impact on others perhaps those in foreign horizons. One may want to listen for the cry of oppression.

One may desire the stability in society promoted by conversation and reciprocal relations not because one is devoted to humanity but because one belongs to the dominant class whose economic interests are served by stability. The shrewdness which recognizes that conversation and some openness to change protects the established order may advance the political interests of the dominant class. The Crits might maintain, then, that destabilization of society by political action through legal argumentation would advance the cause of humanity. In such circumstances, ideological rigidity and rejection of horizon crossing conversation would be desirable.

For those concerned with the cause of humanity as many Crits are, with affording deep respect and concern to each person, or with similar commitments, the ultimate test for the desirability of destabilization would be its impact on human beings. To the extent that destabilization promotes the cause of humanity without seriously violating the basic human dignity of individuals it is desirable. In some circumstances both destabilization and revolution are human responses to impacted oppressive conditions. Wherever the dominant forces in society view rights and legal rules within a single horizon or set of horizons and refuse to engage in conversation, destabilization would seem appropriate;

destabilization in such circumstances becomes a device for breaking through horizons and promoting conversation. However, it may be that stability is a necessary ingredient for normal human existence in community. In a partially just society with open lines of communication more than a moderate amount of destabilization may be anti-human. To the extent that rights perceived within one set of horizons as conclusions drawn within a rigid set of rules are devices for protecting the interests of society's dominant classes they present obstacles to the cause of humanity. To the extent that rights from the perspective of a claimant are a means of hammering on the walls of and penetrating foreign horizons, or from the point of view of the judge are a means for reaching out to the horizons of litigants while crossing or transcending his own, rights discourse would seem to promote the cause of humanity.

The desirability of destabilization and of the preservation or erosion of rights discourse in various circumstances would seem to be appropriate subjects for conversation. To the extent that Dworkin's commitment to friendship and to affording all persons equal respect and concern resembles the commitment of some Crits to civic virtue, to human interconnectedness, or to the cause of humanity it would seem that there is sufficient common ground between their opposing views to provide a basis for such a conversation. If a rigorous concern on Dworkin's part for societal stability or intellectual consistency prevented that more fundamental conversation it would be regrettable. Likewise, it would be unfortunate if devotion to particular ideologies prevented various Crits from addressing deeper questions affecting the cause of humanity. Either of the two failures just described would result from a refusal to cross horizons in intellectual conversation. While at least partial temporary failures of this variety are predictable on both sides, the grand conversation of twentieth century legal philosophy will, of course, continue. That conversation will be enhanced if those of us who share commitments to the cause of humanity, to deep respect and concern for each person, and the like address the questions presented above including the desirability of destabilization, the need for preserving or eroding rights discourse, and the desirability of conversation across intellectual and other horizons. In addressing those questions we could recognize the major contributions of both Dworkin and the Crits to understanding rights discourse and to conducting horizon crossing conversation. We could incorporate the insights of both in our own horizons and relate them to our own deep commitments.

Perhaps the effort to cross political, social, and cultural horizons to discern the impact of law and the structures of society is more important than the intellectual conversation. Pragmatic Instrumentalists have created horizon crossing devices for that purpose. To the extent that Dworkin or the Crits fascinated with the intellectual implications of their own ideological commitments ignore or reject those devices they deviate from a commitment to the cause of humanity, to friendship, to affording all persons equal respect and concern and the like. Judges, scholars, law reformers, or political activists who share those or similar commitments should be concerned with regular crossing of horizons to discern the impact of law, legal decisions, and reform activities or campaigns on those in multiple foreign horizons governed by law or affected by those activities. In other words, in the course of their activities political and legal actors should engage in conversation not only with each other but with those affected by their actions.

D. Rights, Obligations and Deep Commitments--A Hard

Reference Point for Understanding Rights

In the last chapter of this book a model for understanding rights discourse as part of the human struggle was offered in place of a narrow understanding of rights as entitlements, that is rights understood within a single horizon as conclusions drawn within a system of rules. The hard reference point for understanding rights as described in the last chapter of this book was the human struggle, that is the human behavior of establishing, changing, talking about, fighting about, reconciling and struggling with human relations.

Recognition of deep human commitments and their role in rights discourse makes possible a higher interpretation of rights in which the hard reference point is not behavior but obligation grounded in human commitments. Discussion of that higher interpretation should begin with elucidation of the concept of obligation.

Obligation, as H. L. A. Hart explains in *The Concept of Law,*[451] must be distinguished from being obliged for example by an external force such as the threats of a gunman.[452] Rather, an obligation is perceived internally as a reason for one's actions. A person who perceives an obligation to obey a rule, for example, will offer the rule as a reason for his action rather than alleging that he acted from fear of punishment.[453] An observer who is describing the conduct of society from an external point of view may note regularities of behavior from which he may infer the rules of society. However, if the observer really keeps austerely to this extreme external point of view and does not give any account of the manner in which members of the group who accept the rules view their own regular behavior, his description of their life cannot be in terms of rules at all, and so not in the terms of the rule-dependent notions of obligation or duty.[454]

Those who accept rules internally are prepared to offer the rules as reasons justifying their conduct. When one internally perceives a rule, a principle, or a commitment as a compelling reason requiring or justifying conduct one has an obligation.

When one perceives a deep commitment, a background right or an institutional right as a compelling reason for recognizing a concrete right one has an obligation to respect, establish or avoid violating that right. For those who admire philosophical precision, a formula may now be offered: X has a right if Y has an obligation.

The formula just proposed has a familiar ring. Wesley Hohfeld in *Fundamental Legal Conceptions*[455] offered an analysis of jural opposites and jural correlatives.[456] The first set of jural correlatives are right/duty. Where X has a right, Y has a duty.[457] A generation of lawyers found Hohfeld's analysis enlightening.[45]

While the formula offered here resembles Hohfeld's it is different in significant ways. Hohfeld's formula does not account for Hart's understanding of the open texture of law nor for Dworkin's insistence on the importance of deeply held positions for decision making in cases where rules are open textured or his similar insistence on interpretation and Integrity in *Law's Empire.* Hohfeld's formula deals with rights and duties on the rule level and does not address rights and their correlatives in cases where differing conclusions may be reached because the rules are open textured or subject to differing deep interpretation.

In the formula proposed here (and perhaps stolen from Hohfeld and expanded) the word obligation is substituted for the word duty and the formula is stated differently, namely: X has a right if Y has an obligation. In Hohfeld's formula Y who has a duty is typically another litigant or outside of court another citizen who must act in a certain way towards X. For example, if X has a contract right then Y has a duty to perform his contract with X.[459] In the new formula Y who has an obligation may typically be a judge as well as a fellow litigant or citizen. Y's obligation may not be clear on the basis of the relevant rule standing alone because the rule is open textured. Y's obligation becomes clear only after the work of decision making in which Y's deeply held positions are used in arriving at an appropriate conclusion in interpreting the open textured rule. Y's obligation is made up of his deeply held position, his decision making method and their application in arriving at a conclusion.

In the typical application of this new formula X will be a litigant and Y will be a judge. One can say then that X has a right if Y has an obligation to recognize that right. The formula can be applied in a variety of circumstances. For example a law review editor may contend that the courts should recognize a newly proposed right. If the proposed formula were applied in analyzing that contention both X and Y would be hypothetical. Using the formula the contention would be that a litigant X should have the proposed right because a hypothetical judge Y should have an obligation to recognize that right for the reasons stated in the law review note. The law review editor is either proposing a new right or acting as a critic of a court which has rejected the right. Changing point of view slightly one could analyze the statements about rights made by a litigant who is seeking recognition of a new right before a court. Neither X, the litigant, nor the court, Y, are hypothetical. However, X is stating that Y should recognize an obligation to establish that new right for the reasons stated in X's argument. It is correct to conclude that X should have that right if Y has the obligation to recognize it. From the point of view of a judge, X, a litigant, has a right if Y, the judge, perceives an obligation to recognize that right. The judge may employ Dworkin's method for judicial decision making. Under that method the judge will have an obligation to recognize X's right if his deep theory justifies recognition of that right when applied to the interpretation of the institutional concepts. Judge Y_1 may have a deep theory that differs from the deep theory of Judge Y_2. Both theories may support recognition of X's right or one may support recognition of the right while the other leads to rejection of that right. Nevertheless despite the differences between Y_1 and Y_2 the formula applies: X has a right if Y, the judge, perceives an obligation to recognize the right.

The judge, Y, may not accept Dworkin's method for judicial decision making but may hold a deep theory of justice and may use another method for relating that theory to concrete decisions. Again the formula applies: X has a right if Y, the judge perceives an obligation to recognize the right.

The judge, Y, may reject sternly any notion that a deep theory is an appropriate basis for judicial decision making. He may simply apply the rules of law (if that is possible) or may believe that he is simply applying the rules. Judge Y despite Dworkin's arguments to the contrary may be an adherent of majoritarian decision making. Nevertheless Judge Y has a position concerning judicial decision making under which he may perceive an obligation to recognize or reject the claimed right. The formula X has a right if Y the judge recognizes an obligation still applies.

If judge Y is a skeptic he either accepts the legal system and some method of decision making or he decides simply on the basis of his mood of the moment. If he accepts the legal system and a method of decision making then X has a right if under the obligation Judge Y has accepted Y perceives that he should recognize that right. If Y decides only on the basis of his mood of the moment, then, from the perspective of judge Y, X does not have anything that properly could be called a right. Because Y, from his perspective, does not have an obligation X (from that perspective) does not have a right.[460]

The proposed formula appears to be most useful when analyzing statements about rights from the point of view of a judge. The formula seems to work despite the many differing positions that judges may hold concerning judicial methodology or deep theories of justice or government. Furthermore the formula accounts for the possibility that in our pluralistic society one judge may differ from another concerning methodology or deeply held positions.

Nevertheless the formula may be helpful in analyzing academic statements regarding rights. For example one can apply the proposed formula, X has a right if Y has an obligation, in aid of Llewellyn's desire to predict the behavior of judges.[461] While as the realists recognized many factors affect a judge's decision including the quality of his morning cup of coffee, one of the most significant factors is the judge's view of life and law. Those views may arise from the judge's political, social and cultural background. If the court is known and its members have been forthright about their understandings of law and their commitments to deep theories, then, a scholar or lawyer attempting to predict what the court will in fact do is more likely to be correct. Because Y, the judge, has a known obligation it is reasonable to predict that X has a right. A recognition of the role of obligation in judicial decision making and of the different obligations perceived by judges in our pluralist society will enlighten the task of predicting judges' decisions.

When it is not clear that Judge Y's perception of his

obligation will support a finding for X then to that extent from the predictive point of view it is unreasonable to assert that X has a right. Nevertheless it may make sense for a critic from his perspective to state that X has a right. Hart is correct that a prediction that a right will be recognized is not the only meaningful way to talk of rights.[462]

However, recognition of the role of obligation and the proposed formula, X has a right if Y has an obligation, will provide common ground between those taking a predictive point of view and those concerned with describing the use of language in a system of rules. It will also allow us from both of those perspectives to account for and begin to wrestle with the presence of multiple deep views of life and law in our pluralist society.

Likewise, analysis of the dispute between Dworkin and the pragmatic instrumentalists may benefit from the formula. In *Law's Empire*, Dworkin heavily criticizes the theory he describes as Pragmatism.[463] In part, that criticism rests on the disregard by pragmatists of Dworkin's prescription for rigorous consistency in judicial decision making; in part, it rests upon the absence of fundamental moral commitments in pragmatic instrumentalist value theory.[464] Summers, as noted above, also has criticized pragmatic instrumentalist value theory and has suggested that fundamental theories of government or justice could become a basis for choosing between goals in means-goal reasoning.[465] If Summers' suggestion concerning the use of general theory is accepted, then the proposed formula, X has a right where Y has an obligation, may help in reducing conflict between these two methods for judicial decision making.

Under the formula, obligation is the key to the recognition of a right. Judges may be inclined perhaps on the basis of policies, or what they would call policies, to reach a number of decisions. However, from the point of view of the judge, a litigant can be said to have a right to those decisions only where a judge perceives an obligation to reach those conclusions. Some judges, because of their ideology, general theory, or other considerations, will perceive an obligation to support certain group goals which Dworkin would call policies.[466] The right, then, is a right to pursue the goal or have it pursued. Such rights can be distinguished from other policies because the judge, on the basis of a commitment, a theory or otherwise, recognizes an obligation to support certain goals rather than others and to establish concrete rights as means for achieving those goals. Where judge Y perceives an obligation based on his commitment to certain goals, then X, a litigant, has a right which is a means for achievement of the goal.

If the analysis in the last paragraph is correct then Dworkin's insistence in *Taking Rights Seriously* that judges decide on the basis of principle rather than policy[467] may be mistaken. His distinction between principles as reasons based upon individual rights and policies as reasons based on group goals has some usefulness but it should be recognized that some policies may be reasons based on group rights. Where X a litigant can invoke a group right Y a judge may recognize X's right as a means for achieving the goal to which he is committed.

Dworkin may have difficulty accepting this analysis because his own liberal ideology places a heavy emphasis on individual rights. However, his method for decision making is formal in the sense that it can be used by judges who hold many different fundamental theories some of which may have an important place for such societal goals as economic development. Dworkin's method in *Taking Rights Seriously* and probably also in *Law's Empire* may be useful to more judges in our pluralist society if the distinction between principles and policies is drawn less tightly and the possibility is recognized that some judges who want to take rights seriously will rest their decisions on group rights and other policies. It is possible to develop an interpretation of law which would encompass decisions based on policy as well as principles.

As suggested earlier in the book one could capture Dworkin's desire to protect individual rights in preference to group goals better by using Rawls' method of lexical ordering.[468] A judge (perhaps Hercules) could decide on the basis of principle or policy while insisting that strong individual rights have lexical priority over strong group goals. He could, of course, have a more complex lexical ordering preferring first strong individual rights, second strong group rights and third other goals and policies. Each judge's lexical ordering would rest on his general theory of law. While accepting at Dworkin's suggestion the need for a general theory, and the need to afford strong protection to individual rights a judge who believes that he is taking rights seriously could rest many decisions on policy and use the pragmatic instrumentalist method of means-goal reasoning.[469]

The key to this proposed reconciliation of Dworkin and pragmatic instrumentalist method is the notion of obligation. If Judge Y recognizes an obligation to support a group goal then X in appropriate circumstances will have a right. Under a particular judge's theory recognition of group goals may be important to taking rights seriously.

One can push the argument one step further. A pragmatic instrumentalist judge who uses means-goal reasoning exclusively and who does not recognize an obligation to any goal never perceives an obligation to arrive at any particular decision. Such a judge is not able to take rights seriously. Since pragmatic instrumentalist courts have established many important constitutional rights it is probable that many such judges held strong commitments to group goals or to fundamental theories which would support those rights. Summers' suggestion that fundamental theory be joined to pragmatic instrumentalist method as a basis for choosing between goals[470] may be a codification and improvement of some past practice.

Judge Posner with his rejection of overarching theory and his insistence that the ordinary methods of legal reasoning[471] provide no serious justification for decisions may be perceived by some critics as a pragmatic instrumentalist judge who is not able to take rights seriously. That criticism would overlook his continual references to the importance of his oath to uphold the Constitution. In the vast number of routine cases he normally would employ ordinary legal reasoning. Posner then usually would protect the "legal rights" which Dworkin is concerned with in *Law's Empire* as well as more important Constitutional rights. Using the predictive approach of Llewellyn and Holmes, litigants before Judge Posner would have rights because they could make a fair prediction that the judge would afford them a remedy. Posner's own discussion does not appear to use the high pretense which Dworkin attributes to some pragmatists of acting "as if" there were rights while ultimately denying those rights. Rather, he appears to be describing his understanding or interpretation of the role of a conscientious judge. To the extent that he accepts that role then X, the litigants before him, have rights because Y, the judge accepts an obligation.

One could raise a similar set of questions in regard to those members of the Critical Legal Studies Movement who have criticized rights discourse.[472] If a Crit were to become a judge could he take rights seriously? Under the analysis offered above[473] arguably he would take some rights seriously. Some Crits would have strong ideological commitments or strong commitments to the cause of humanity. On the basis of those commitments their decisions in a range of cases would be fairly predictable. Using the predictive analysis of Holmes and Llewellyn a number of litigants would have rights because they could predict that the judge would afford a remedy.[474] Using the formula X has a right if Y has an obligation from a number of different points of view the Crit as judge could be said to respect rights whether he uses rights or anti-rights rhetoric. The stronger his acceptance and adherence to his ideology, the stronger the commitment which would support some rights for some X's. Granted, however, that some X's would not have the rights before the Crit as judge that they normally would expect. Nevertheless, some Crits would accept aspects of the role of judge that would allow them to transcend their ideological horizons. Duncan Kennedy, for example, in his article, "Freedom and Constraint in Adjudication: A Critical Phenomenology",[475] expresses a normal commitment to make only those decisions which he can support by good legal argument. He also indicates that he may be persuaded by the wisdom found in precedents that are at odds with his ideological positions.

Under the formula, X has a right if Y has an obligation, one can recognize a right by asking if anyone existing or hypothetical has or perceives an obligation to recognize it. Obligation is the touchstone of right. From any particular point of view a right exists if Y from that perspective perceives an obligation to accept or establish the right. In our pluralist society there will be many different views and understanding of rights because there are many different understandings of obligation based upon multiple deep views of life and law.

Nevertheless, under the proposed formula each of the statements about rights listed at the beginning of the book[476] may in appropriate circumstances describe rights properly so called. As already noted rights are conclusions drawn within a system of open textured rules when the one drawing the conclusion, judge, critic or claimant can state (probably using a deep theory) that Y has an obligation in the formula X has a right if Y has an obligation.[477] Y in some of these statements may be hypothetical. Rights are remedies which a court predictably will grant where the one making the prediction can fairly state that the court will perceive an obligation supporting the remedy.[478]

From the perspective of a deciding judge rights are trumps when he perceives an obligation to recognize them despite competing considerations and arguments including perhaps arguments of policy.[479] Rights are reasons from the perspective of a deciding judge when he has accepted an obligation perhaps based on a deep theory to take those rights seriously and to reach holdings in appropriate circumstances which are supported by those reasons.[480]

Likewise goals are rights when someone perceives an obligation perhaps under a deep theory to pursue those goals.[481] Under means-goal reasoning a goal right can become a reason for the pursuit of other more concrete rights and from the perspective of a deciding judge for reaching a holding establishing a concrete right. Indeed, a goal right can become a trump when someone interfering with the pursuit of a goal is sued by those injured by the interference. When such a dispute arises in court, the right to pursue the goal may become a reason for a holding which will trump competing reasons. More often, however, a goal right is not a trump because a court cannot direct that an important goal such as economic development be pursued to the exclusion of other goals. Nevertheless where one perceives an obligation to pursue the goal perhaps while engaged in other endeavors the goal is a right.

Rights become resources because someone perceives an obligation to recognize them.[482] An interest group confronting society may use a claim of right in the course of that confrontation to gather adherents and attack opponents. In analyzing a claim of right including one used by an interest group as a political resource, one would state that X has a right because a hypothetical Y should have an obligation. Under Scheingold's analysis a claim of right becomes an effective resource when it is supported by the American myth of rights or when the public's understanding of the myth of rights can be expanded to include the claimed right.[483] In other words the right is effective as a political resource when the public in general recognizes a generalized obligation to accept that right or when it is fairly predictable that the public may be persuaded to recognize a generalized obligation to accept the right. To the extent that it is not reasonable to make that prediction the right is a less effective resource.

When Judge Y has a strong ideological commitment, a litigant X has a right when his desired result is supported by that ideology. When a law reformer committed to a strong ideology is seeking to change society, then whether he uses rights or anti-rights rhetoric he is promoting the rights of those groups or individuals who would benefit from his ideological goals. From his perspective as a critic and claimant, he is arguing that X should receive certain benefits or results because Y a hypothetical judge or legislator should accept an obligation ultimately supported by the law reformer's ideology.[484]

Rights as rhetoric succeed in a complex pluralist society

composed of multiple horizons when they appeal to the commitments or obligations of those in other horizons.[485] Those commitments or obligations may be expanded to include the proposed rights by a persuasive sharing of experience perhaps supported by narration. Ultimately through the rhetoric of a long law reform campaign obligations in general may be expanded as Scheingold indicated by expansion of the myth of rights. The high argument and conversation of law as rhetoric succeeds best in holding society together and constituting it when it is a successful sharing of experience between those with deep understandings of life and law including deep commitments and obligations who have arrived at their understandings in the context of different horizons.

Using obligation as a touchstone for identifying rights and stating that, in the formula, X has a right if Y has an obligation offers the possibility of clarifying some disputes between those making statements about rights. It appears to clarify the now ancient confrontation between Hart and the legal realists as well as the current discussion between Dworkin and the pragmatic-instrumentalists. Since the formula can be applied to the various statements about rights made at the beginning of the book it offers the possibility for further unification of the discussion of rights.

In a pluralist society it may be very helpful to understand statements about rights as related to multiple deep views of life and law. Using obligations as a touchstone of rights in the formula X has a right if Y has an obligation relates every statement of right to someone's understanding of obligation perhaps an understanding which is based on a deep view of life and law. Each statement of right, then, has a reference point in someone's understanding of obligation, perhaps a well worked out understanding of obligation based on a deep theory. We can understand the limitations on and the force of each statement of right by asking who accepts the correlative obligation and how significant those who accept that obligation are for the particular discussion or decision. Thc proposed formula is a means for analyzing rights that is analogous to Hart's statement that rights are conclusions drawn within a system of rules[486] and to Dworkin's view in *Taking Rights Seriously* that those conclusions in a system of open textured rules may rest on deep positions[487] or his view in *Law's Empire* that our decisions result from interpretations of law that should make the most of our institutions.[488] The proposed formula extends a similar analysis to a wider range of statements about rights.

The presence of disputes about rights in a pluralist society based on multiple deep views of life and law rather than rendering the discussion of rights meaningless indicates that we are heavily engaged in multiple and continuing conversations about rights and in an effort to convey our understanding of rights to each other. Many of the statements about rights are grounded in an understanding of obligation perhaps a highly systematized understanding of obligation. The acceptance of obligation by various role players or groups in society has actual results in the recognition of rights of other parties and in the establishment of relations in society. And as James Boyd White argues, the high argument between those with differing deep positions or interpretations of life and law may constitute society.[489] It certainly assists in holding society together.

Overview and Conclusion

H. L. A. Hart took as one of his projects the creation of great clarifying concepts which would allow us to describe law wherever it is found. In that sense, this book has offered an analytical framework and a series of clarifying concepts which may be helpful in describing and understanding rights discourse in a pluralist society, a society composed of multiple horizons. In contrast to Hart's understanding of law as a system of rules, it also has offered a vision of law as an activity in which the language of rights is used as one set of tools for conducting human relations. The Grand Conversation of twentieth century American legal philosophy is an illustration of that vision as is the large progress made in the course of the twentieth century in establishing, advancing and arguing about human and constitutional rights.

The early chapters (I and II) of this book[490] report, reflect on and begin the process of reconciling conflicting accounts about the uses of rights. Recounting the spectrum of views in regard to one aspect of jurisprudential thought, namely rights, offers what could be described as a biopsy of twentieth century jurisprudence. The report offers an opportunity for insight into various jurisprudential views and their relation to each other in what has been described as a Grand Conversation. Beyond that the catalog and discussion of the multiple uses of rights illustrates the departure from a simple model of rights as entitlements, that is, rights as conclusions drawn within a system of rules and within a single horizon without explicit reference to the use of those rights from different perspectives or the points of view of different law jobs. Indeed, after reviewing multiple uses of rights as perceived in the horizons of different jurisprudential views it is apparent that our understanding of rights discourse has advanced far beyond that simple model usable in a formalist understanding of law. The comparisons and contrasts between various jurisprudential views offers a foundation for tracing and recreating the Grand Conversation of twentieth century jurisprudence and for recognizing the genuine contributions of the various participants to our understanding of rights.

In the course of tracing the Grand Conversation, we were able to recognize and reflect on some of the techniques for conversation, particularly those used by H. L. A. Hart but also those contributed by Ronald Dworkin and James Boyd White among others. An important aspect of those techniques is the ability to recognize the genuine insights offered by an opposing view, followed by extraction of those insights and incorporation of them into one's own understanding. Drawing upon the insights of others this book offers another important aspect of conversation, namely the techniques for crossing and transcending horizons. Point of View Analysis and Horizon Analysis in addition are techniques for understanding rights statements and in regard to academic discussions of rights for locating and extracting the genuine good sense and insights from the almost necessarily limited horizons of a particular academic analysis. Those insights then are available for use in other horizons in furtherance of the Grand Conversation.

There are three major aspects of this book, the report and analysis of the Grand Conversation,[491] the model for understanding rights discourse,[492] and the presentation and application of the formula, X has a right if Y has an obligation.[493] A question which arises almost as a theme from the Grand Conversation, namely, are statements and arguments regarding rights meaningful in view of the multiple understandings and uses of rights, unites all three major aspects of the book.

Offering a simple model in answer to that question is impossible after following the Grand Conversation. We have departed too far from the simplicity of early formalism. It was submitted in the course of discussion that rejection of rights discourse as meaningless is also too simplistic. Rather the use of point of view and horizon analysis can extract the good sense from rights statements made from particular perspectives and within foreign horizons. A more complex model was offered for understanding rights statements.[494] In that model it is recognized (1) that law is not merely open textured but often radically open textured, (2) that every statement, including every statement regarding rights is made within a horizon and, (3) from a point of view and further (4) that every rights statement is made from an academic perspective or for one or more of the purposes described in the catalog of the uses of rights. One should recognize that academic statements, for example, those reported in this book, often track uses of rights outside the academic setting. In our society, a pluralist society composed of multiple horizons, statements and arguments are often made across horizons with a view to appealing to or calling for recognition from those in foreign horizons.

Llewellyn and Hart both were concerned with hard reference points for rights discourse. The model offered in this book for understanding rights discourse has a hard reference point, namely the behavior in our pluralist society of those engaged in rights discourse, and behavior in which we use rights discourse and indeed sometimes anti-rights discourse to establish, change, talk about, fight about, reconcile and struggle with human relations.

There is a higher hard reference point, namely obligation. To the extent that a judge has an obligation the litigants before him have rights and he is capable of taking rights seriously. The formula, X has a right if Y has an obligation allows an analysis and interpretation of rights statements and rights discourse. The formula is most appropriately used in connection with the model for understanding rights discourse and together with the model offers an analysis of rights discourse in which the question whether statements and arguments regarding rights are meaningful in view of the multiple uses of rights receives a complex but affirmative answer. In view of the formula any particular person may reflect on his own horizons, deeper obligations, and explore the foundations for rights more deeply. The formula also offers a further basis for analysis of conversations using rights discourse across horizons in a pluralist society. Rights discourse as a horizon crossing device will be most effective when it appeals to another's obligations as perceived within his horizon. One may have to expand the listener's horizons in the course of argument in order to accomplish that perhaps by joining rights discourse with narration. The formula further offers a foundation for analyzing rights discourse and conversation as the rhetoric that constitutes society. In a pluralist society arguments across horizons about what society should be using rights discourse among other means not only promotes the stability of society but at times relates those engaged in the discourse and the interests and groups they represent as persons sharing experience.

Beyond the question of the meaningfulness of rights

discourse in a pluralist society and the presentation of the model and formula to analyze and respond to that question the book offers suggestions regarding judicial decisions, the development of theories regarding judicial decision making and the reconciliation of jurisprudential views. This is a side product of the analysis. The book is about the language and uses of rights and not directly about methods of judicial decision making. Nevertheless the methods for analyzing rights statements and for transcending and crossing horizons generate suggestions for judicial decision making and offer possibilities for extracting insights from various jurisprudential positions which possibly may be related to insights from competing positions much in the manner of H. L. A. Hart. For example, Dworkin's use of deep positions and the process of interpretation which relates them to law could be used in conjunction with pragmatic instrumentalist method. James Boyd White's understanding of law as rhetoric could be related to Dworkin's understanding of interpretation and to the definition in this book of a pluralist society as one made up of multiple horizons.

The point of view adopted in this book is largely descriptive and analytical and only occasionally prescriptive. Among the prescriptions worth reiterating are the insistence on conversation, on the importance of crossing and transcending horizons and ultimately on the importance of understanding rights in relation to people. Those with a commitment to affording all persons deep respect and concern or to the cause of humanity should delight in the multiple ways in which rights are used in the game of life to establish, change, talk about, fight about, reconcile and struggle with human relations.

Notes

I. Purposes and Basic Insights

1. *Cf.* Donnelly, "Principles, Persons and Horizons: A Friendly Analysis of What Dworkin Has Overlooked" *26 St. Louis U.L.J.* 217, 217-20 (1982) [hereinafter Donnelly].
2. *See, e.g.*, Hart, "Definition and Theory in Jurisprudence," 70 *Law. Q. Rev.* 37 (1954) [hereinafter "Definition and Theory']; Fuller, "Positivism and Fidelity to Law--a Reply to Professor Hart," 71 *Harv. L. Rev.* 630 (1958) [hereinafter "Fidelity to Law"]; Hart, "Positivism and the Separation of Law and Morals," 71 *Harv. L. Rev.* 593 (1958) [hereinafter "Separation of Law and Morals"]; (Although Hart is British, any analysis of American Jurisprudence must contain his influential contributions to the field in general); *See, e.g.*, Lon Fuller, *The Morality of Law* (1964); Lon Fuller, *Anatomy of Law* (1968); *See, e.g.*, Dworkin, Hard Cases" 88 *Harv. L. Rev.* 1057 (1975) [hereinafter "Hard Cases"]; Hart, "American Jurisprudence Through English Eyes: The Nightmare and The Noble Dream" 11 *Ga. L. Rev.* 969 [hereinafter "Noble Dream"] 984-85 (1977); Dworkin, "Seven Critics" 11 Ga. *L. Rev.* 1201 (1977) [hereinafter "Seven Critics"]; Dworkin "No Right Answer" 53 *N.Y.U. L. Rev.* 1 (1978) [hereinafter No Right Answer].
3. Critical legal thinkers emerged in the late 1970's. Some of the notable leaders of this movement include: Duncan Kennedy, Morton Horwitz, Karl Klare, Mark Tushnet and Roberto Unger. In recent years, these leading Crits have been joined by a cast of thousands. "The work of the critical legal scholars can be understood as the maturation of ... Realist methodologies" toward iconoclastic historiography and rigorous analytic jurisprudence," A maturation in which critical legal scholars explore incoherences at the level of social or political theory and critical scholarship is linked, not to reformist programs, but to a radical political agenda." Note, 'Round and 'Round

the Bramble Bush: From Legal Realism to Critical Legal Scholarship, 95 *Harv. L. Rev.* 1669, 1676-77 (1982). See, Roberto Mangabeira Unger, The Critical Legal Studies Movement 96 *Harv. L. Rev.* 563 (1983). See also, "Critical Legal Studies Symposium" 36 *Stan. L. Rev.* 1 (1984); Horwitz, "The Bork Nomination and American Constitutional History" (Kharas Lecture Series) 39 *Syracuse L. Rev.* 1027 (1988).

4. *See, e.g.*, West, "The Differences in Women's Hedonic Lives" A Phenomenological Critique of Feminist Legal Theory," 3 *Wis. Women's L.J.* 80 (1987); West "Jurisprudence and Gender," 55 *U. Chi. L. Rev.* 1 (1988); *See also*, Martha Minow, *Making All the Difference: Inclusion, Exclusion and American Law* (1990).

5."Outsider Jurisprudence focuses on the failure of traditional-neutral-jurisprudence to achieve true equality for oppressed groups." Note, "Racist Speech, The First Amendment, and Public Universities: Taking a Stand on Neutrality," 76 *Cornell L. Rev.* 549,571-73 (1991); In Mari J. Mastuda's Writings "Outsider" is used to avoid "minority" a term that belies the numerical significance of the constituencies typically excluded from jurisprudential discourse. *See, e.g.*, Mastuda, "Public Response to Racist Speech: Considering the Victim's Story," 87 *Mich. L. Rev.* 2320, 2323-24 (1989).

6. *See* James Boyd White, *Heracles' Bow Essays on the Rhetoric and Poetics of the Law*(1985). [hereinafter *Heracles' Bow*]

7. *See* Posner, "The Ethical and Political Basis of the Efficiency Norm in Common Law Adjudicaiton,: 8 *Hofstra L. Rev* 487 (1980); See Richard Posner, *The Economics of Justice* (1981); See West, "Authority, Autonomy, And Choice: The Role of Consent in the Moral and Political Visions of Franz Kafka and Richard Posner" 99 *Harv. L. Rev.* 384 (1985); See Posner, "The Ethical Significance of Free Choice: A Reply to Professor West" 99 *Harv. L. Rev.* 1431 (1986); *See* West, "Submission, Choice, and Ethics: A Rejoinder to Judge Posner," 99 *Harv. L. Rev.* 1449 (1986); *See* Richard Posner, *Law and Literature: A Misunderstood Relation* (1988); *See* West, "Law, Literature, and the Celebration of Authority (Bork Review Exchange)" 83 *NW U. L. Rev.* 977 (1989); *See* Richard Posner, *The Problems of Jurisprudence* 225, 231, 389, 409-413 (1990), *See* R. Posner, *Sex and Reason* (1992).

8. One may read this book as an analysis of the way the language of rights is used in legal or related discussions. However, language analysis can reveal human behavior and provide a basis for a deeper understanding of human relations. Analysis of the language of rights,

can reveal a number of ways in which the players in society use rights to advance interests, make claims, establish relations and carry forward conversations.

9. *See* H.L.A. Hart, "Definition and Theory in Jurisprudence" 70 *Law Q. Rev.* 37, 43 (1954) [hereinafter Definition and Theory]..

10. *See* Llewellyn, *Jurisprudence Realism in Theory and Practice* 3-41 (1962) [hereinafter *Jurisprudence], c.f.* Llewellyn "A Realist Jurisprudence--The Next Step" 30 *Colum. L. Rev.* 431 (1930); *See Jurisprudence* 42-74; *c.f.* Llewellyn "Some Realism about Realism--Responding to Dean Pound," 44 *Harv. L. Rev.* 1222 (1931); Llewellyn states that legal realism is not a school, thus all legal realists may not support his position. However, both Llewellyn and legal realist Jerome Frank do follow this view. *See Jurisprudence* 21-22; *See also* J. Frank, *Courts on Trial* 5-13 (1950) [hereinafter *Courts on Trial*].

11. R. Dworkin, *Taking Rights Seriously* 17-22, 82-90 (1977) [hereinafter *Taking Rights Seriously*]; No Right Answer *supra* note 2, *Hard Cases supra* note 2.

12. *See Moore v. East Cleveland*, 431 U.S. 494 (1977) (right of members of extended family to live together); *Duncan v. Louisiana*, 391 U.S. 145 (1968) (right to an impartial jury).

13. *See, e.g., Woodson v. North Carolina*, 428 U.S. 280 (1976) (the Supreme Court has rejected mandatory death penalty schemes); *Coker v. Georgia*, 433 U.S. 584 (1977) (the court held that the death penalty was excessive punishment for the crime of rape of an adult woman).

14. *See supra* notes 12, 13.

15. *Taking Rights Seriously supra* note 11 at 93; See S. Donnelly, A Theory of Justice, Judicial Methodology, and the Constitutionality of Capital Punishment: Rawls, Dworkin, and a Theory of Criminal Responsibility, 29 *Syr. L. R.* 1109, 1114-15 (1978) [hereinafter cited as Constitutionality of Capital Punishment].

16. *See* Ronald Dworkin, *Law's Empire* (1986) [hereinafter *Law's Empire*].

17. *Universal Declaration of Human Rights,* Dec. 10, 1948, G.A. Res. 217 A (III), U.N. Doc.A/810, at 71 (1948), [hereinafter *Declaration of Human Rights*].

18. See R. Summers, *Instrumentalism and American Legal Theory* 60-66 (1982) [hereinafter cited as *Summers*].

19. See *Brown v. Board of Education*, 347 U.S. 483, 494-5 (1954).

The Court concluded "that in the field of public education the doctrine of 'separate but equal' has no place." *Id.* at 495. This decision was based upon findings that the segregation of public schools failed to provide equal educational opportunities for equally qualified children.
20. "The Constitutional safeguard, we have said, was fashioned to assure unfettered interchange of ideas for the bringing about of political and social changes desired by the people?" *New York Times v. Sullivan,* 376 U.S. 254, 269 (1963); *quoting Roth v. United States*, 354 U.S. 476, 484 (1956).
21. *New York Times v. Sullivan*, 376 U.S. 254, 270. The court states "Thus we consider this case against the background of a profound national commitment to the principle that debate on public issues should be uninhibited, robust, and wide-open," at 270.
22. Definition and Theory, *supra* note 9 at 42.
23. *Id.* at 44.
24. S. Scheingold, *The Politics of Rights* 83-84 (1974) [hereinafter *Scheingold*].
25. *See* Unger, "The Critical Legal Studies Movement, 96 *Harv. L. Rev*. 561, 597 (1983); Tushnet, "Following the Rules Laid Down: A Critique of Interpretivism and Neutral Principles," 96 *Harv. L. Rev*. 781 (1983); Tushnet, "An Essay on Rights," 62 *Tex. L. Rev*. 1363 (1984); Horwitz, "The Bork Nomination and American Constitutional History" 39 *Syracuse L. Rev*. 1029 (1988).
26. Hart, "Separation of Law and Morals," *supra* note 2 at 615-21; cf. Hart, "Definition and Theory," *supra* note 2.
27. *See* Tushnet, "An Essay on Rights" 62 *Texas L. Rev*. 1363 (1984).
28. *See infra* text accompanying notes 242-78.
29. Kennedy, "Freedom and Constraint in Adjudication: A Critical Phenomenology" 36 *J. Legal Educ*. 518 (1986) [hereinafter Kennedy].
30. *Id.* at 524-25.
31. Roberto Mangabeira Unger, "The Critical Legal Studies Movement" 96 *Harv. L. Rev*. 563, 599-600 (1983). [hereinafter Critical Legal Studies Movement].
32. *See supra* text accompanying notes 25-31.
33. *Heracles' Bow supra* note 4 at xii, 28, 32-35, 37.
34. *See* West, "Jurisprudence as Narration" at *supra* note 5. See West, "The Supreme Court, 1989 Term, Taking Freedom Seriously," 104 *Harv. L. Rev*. 43, 85-93 (1990).
35. *See* Donnelly *supra* note 1 at 254 n. 250. *See also infra* notes

289-316 and accompanying text.
36. *See supra* text accompanying notes 9-34.
37. *See infra* text accompanying notes 317-21.
38. *See infra* text accompanying notes 416-489.
39. *See infra* text accompanying notes 418-442.
40. *See infra* text accompanying notes 416-489.

II. The Grand Conversation

41. *See, e.g.*, Llewellyn *Jurisprudence supra* note 10 at 3-42; *c.f.* Llewellyn, "A Realist Jurisprudence--The Next Step," 30 *Colum. L. Rev.* 431 (1930); *See also Jurisprudence supra* note 10 at 42-76, *c.f.* Llewellyn "Some Realism About Realism--Responding to Dean Pound," 44 *Harv. L. Rev.* 1222 (1931).
42. *See supra* text accompanying notes 7-34.
43. *See infra* text accompanying notes 287-414.
44. *See* Donnelly *supra* note 1 at 217-18. Much of the conversation is due to the effort of H. L. A. Hart. His exchanges with Lon Fuller and with the Scandinavian Legal Realists are well known. One could argue that some of his basic concepts are an attempt to relate analytical thought to American Legal Realism. His contention that legal rules have and ought to have an open texture could be understood as an effort to rescue and order some of the insights which emerged as rule skepticism in legal realist thought. Open textured rules will have a virtually undisputed core meaning and will be accompanied by a shadow or penumbral area in which the rule may or may not apply. Under one meaning of Hart's view, a judge settling a dispute covered by the core meaning of a rule simply applies the rule. If the dispute arises over the application of the rule in its penumbral area, the judge has discretion in its strong sense to apply or not apply the rule. Another important clarifying concept offered by Hart is that a legal system is composed of the union of primary rules of obligation and secondary rules about primary rules such as rules of recognition, change, and adjudication. One could argue that this concept is designed not merely to correct some deficiencies in Austin's understanding of law but also to deal with the legal realist notion that law is continually in flux. *Id.*
45. Definition and Theory, *supra* note 9.
46. *See* W. Twining, *Karl Llewellyn and the Realist Movement* (1973) [hereinafter cited as *Twining*]. Summers, *supra* note 18.
47. H. L. A. Hart, *The Concept of Law*, 126 (1961) [hereinafter

Concept of Law]. Hart goes on to explain how one may achieve a formalistic system. Hart offers us a mechanical approach. First, we determine the meaning of the rule by looking at what constitutes the general terms of the rule. This requires a conceptualization of a set of necessary and sufficient conditions that will give the general terms their meaning. This allows us to fix the general terms to a single meaning. Second, we determine whether the case before us contains the same essential elements as the general terms. If the case before us has the same necessary and sufficient features as the general term, then the rule applies. The rule applies regardless of the underlying policies or the effects on the individuals. Hart explains that formalism gives us the luxury of predictability and certainty; however, this comes "at the cost of blindly prejudging what is to be done in a range of future cases, about whose composition we are ignorant." *Id.* at 126.

Hart explains that the mathematical approach of formalism will require us to include cases that we would be inclined to exclude. The flexibility that open textured language offers will be sacrificed for certainty and predictability. Thus, we may have to abandon the policies and concerns that underlie the rule in order to fulfill the rigid requirements of a formalistic approach. Id. at 126-27; *see also Twining supra* note 46 at 41-55; *see also Summers supra* note 18 at 136-176.

48. See W. Wiecek, *Constitutional Development in a Modernizing Society: The United States, 1803 to 1917*, (1985). He states,

> Formalism was not so much a coherent jurisprudential philosophy as a set of assumptions about the way human society functioned. Formalist judges sought to achieve justice by abstracting the essential legal relationship from all the human circumstances of a case and impersonally applying existing law - law that they had 'found' rather than created - to that relationship, undistorted by human bias and prejudice...
>
> A formalist judge could not let himself picture the human reality of an immigrant Hungarian steelworker and the United States Steel Corporation with the obvious, gross disparity in stature and power between them. *Id.* at 59; see also W. Wiecek, "*A Great and Stately Jurisdiction*, (unpublished manuscript). He states, concerning 19th century formalist judges: "To

> them, however, what they called 'legal science' was timeless, classical in its harmony, balance and logic. Their methodological base was an approach to law that we call formalism, a way of doing law that was more a method than a coherent philosophy...
> Benedict insists that judges did not cynically manipulate this ideological bent to cover or rationalize their solicitude for the haves in their struggle with the have-nots...
> But of course we see it differently a century later. Formalism was so obviously allied with conservative social and economic bias that its pretensions to neutrality, autonomy, and justice seem to us a hypocritical sham.

49. *See Twining supra* note 46 at 8-9; *Summers supra* note 16 at 137-159.
50. K. Llewellyn, *The Common Law Tradition: Deciding Appeals* 62-120 (1960) [hereinafter *The Common Law Tradition]; C.f. Jurisprudence, supra* note 10 at 215-29.
51. *See Jurisprudence, supra* note 10 at 21-27.
52. Holmes, "The Path of the Law," 10 *Harv. L. Rev.* 457, 461 (1897); see *Jurisprudence, supra* note 10 at 22.
53. *Jurisprudence, supra* note 10 at 23-25.
54. *Twining supra* note 46 at 188-190; *Jurisprudence supra* note 10 at 55-56.
55. *Cf. Summers supra* note 16 at 161-166.
56. *Cf. The Concept of Law supra* note 47 at 121-132.
57. *Id.* at 132-144.
58. *Id.* at 144.
59. *Id.*
60. *See* text accompanying note 50; *Cf. The Concept of Law supra* note 47 at 121-32.
61. *The Concept of Law, supra* note 47, at 124-25.
62. *Id.* at 123-132.
63. *Id.* at 123, 132.
64. *Jurisprudence, supra* note 10 at 8-14, 23-27.
65. *Id.* at 22; *Courts on Trial, supra* note 10 at 9.
66. *The Common Law Tradition, supra* note 10 at 399-400.
67. Inaugural lecture delivered before the University of Oxford on May

30, 1953. Definition and Theory, *supra* note 9 at 37, 41-49.
68. *See id.* at 38-41.
69. *See Jurisprudence*, *supra* note 10 at 12-13.
70. See Definition and Theory, *supra* note 9 at 42.
71. *Id.* at 49.
72. *Id.* at 42-45.
73. *Id.* at 43-44.
74. *Id.* at 42; *see also Concept of Law supra* note 47 at 138-41.
75. *See* "Definition and Theory" *supra* note 2 at 43-44; *see also Concept of Law supra* note 47 at 10-11.
76. See Donnelly, *supra* note 1 at 218; Dworkin, *Taking Rights Seriously, supra* note 11 at 7-13; "Hard Cases" *supra* note 2; *The Concept of Law supra* note 74; "Separation of Law and Morals" *supra* note 2; "Noble Dream" *supra* note 2; "Seven Critics" *supra* note 2; *Law's Empire supra* note 16 at 33-35; 114-150.
77. *See Taking Rights Seriously, supra* note 11 at 131-149.
78. *See, e.g.*, A. Bickel, *The Least Dangerous Branch; The Supreme Court at the Bar of Politics* (1962) [hereinafter cited as *Bickel*]; H. Wechsler, *Toward Neutral Principles of Constitutional Law*, 73 *Harv. L. Rev.* 1 (1959) [hereinafter cited as *Wechsler*].
79. *Id.*
80. *Taking Rights Seriously*, *supra* note 11 at 84-88, 131-49.
81. *Law's Empire, supra* note 16 at 33-35, 114-50.
82. *Id.* at 378, *see* also Id. at 369-379.
83. *Taking Rights Seriously*, *supra* note 11 at 85.
84. *Id.* at 82-84.
85. *Id.* at 85.
86. *Id.* at 82-84.
87. *Taking Rights Seriously, supra* note 11.
88. *Id.* at 81.
89. *Summers, supra* note 18 at 167, 176-190.
90. Donnelly, *supra* note 1 a 291-92.
91. Definition and Theory, *supra* note 9 at 43.
92. *Cf. Taking Rights Seriously, supra* note 11 at 81-130.
93. *The Concept of Law, supra* note 68 at 120-132.
94. *Id.*
95. *See Taking Rights Seriously, supra* note 11 at 81-149.
96. *See, Id.* at 135.
97. *See, Id.* at 88, 116.

98. *See, Id.* at 86-88, 106-107.
99. *See, Taking Rights Seriously, supra* note 11 at 88, 116.
100. *Id.* at 82, 91.
101. *Id.* at 93.
102. *Id.*
103. *See, e.g., Hutto v. Finney,* 437 U.S. 678 (1978).
104. U. S. Const. amend. VIII.
105. *Taking Rights Seriously, supra* note 11 at 93-94.
106. *See* Donnelly, "A Theory of Justice, Judicial Methodology, and the Constitutionality of Capital Punishment: Rawls, Dworkin, and a Theory of Criminal Responsibility," 29 Syracuse L. Rev. 1109, 1130 (1978) [hereinafter Constitutionality of Capital Punishment].
107. *Taking Rights Seriously, supra* note 11 at 84.
108. *Id.* at 86-88, 106-107.
109. *Constitutionality of Capital Punishment, supra* note 106 at 1130.
110. *Id.*
111. *See, Taking Rights Seriously, supra* note 11 at 88, 116.
112. *See, Id.* at 116; see also, Donnelly, *supra* note 1 at 234-35.
113. *Taking Rights Seriously, supra* note 11 at 86-88; Donnelly, *supra* note 1 at 224-25.
114. *See, Taking Rights Seriously, supra* note 11 at 93; *see,* Donnelly supra note 1 at 222.
115. *See Id.*
116. *See Id.*
117. *Taking Rights Seriously, supra* note 11 at 94-96.
118. *Taking Rights Seriously, supra* note 11 at 81-130.
119. *See, supra* text accompanying note 93-98; *cf, Taking Rights Seriously, supra* note 11 at 132-137.
120. *See, The Concept of Law, supra* note 47 at 132; "Separation of Law and Morals," *supra* note 2 at 610.
121. *See supra* note 107-112 and accompanying text; *cf. Taking Rights Seriously, supra* note 11 at 82.
122. *Taking Rights Seriously, supra* note 11 at 82-84.
123. *Taking Rights Seriously, supra* note 11.
124. *See, The Concept of Law, supra* note 47 at 131-32; see also "Separation of Law and Morals" *supra* note 2 at 612, 626, 629; *see also, Taking Rights Seriously, supra* note 11 at 82.
125. *Taking Rights Seriously, supra* note 11 at 101-105.
126. *See, e.g.,* Hart, "Noble Dream," *supra* note 2, *see e.g., Dworkin,*

"Seven Critics," supra note 2 (reprinted with modification in *Taking Rights Seriously, supra* note 11, see generally *supra* note 1.

127. *Cf. Summers, supra* note 18.

128. *Law's Empire, supra* note 16.

129. *Law's Empire, supra* note 16 at 45-87.

130. *Id., see Id.* at 37-44.

131. *Law's Empire, supra* note 16 at 114-150 (Discussion of conventionalism as an interpretive theory).

132. Dworkin identifies three stages in what he calls "constructive interpretation." In a "preinterpretive stage" there is a general consensus on the materials of law. *Law's Empire, supra* note 16 at 65. Dworkin goes on to describe the second and third stages of interpretation. He describes the second stage as one where "the interpreter settles on some general justification for the main elements of the practice identified at the preinterpretive stage." *Id.* at 65. This stage requires the interpreter to offer a justification of the primary elements of the social practice. This does not involve a defense of every nuance of the practice; rather, the interpreter must only feel an alliance to its central precepts. The second stage, then, is an appreciation of enough of the general ideas behind a practice so that it is clear the interpreter is talking about the same shared social practice and not inventing a new one. Dworkin describes the third stage as the reform or postinterpretive stage. It is at this point that the interpreter "adjusts his sense of what the practice `really' requires so as better to serve the justification he accepts at the interpretive stage." *Id.* at 65. The reform stage requires an evaluation of the details in an effort to make the practice congruent to its general purposes. Thus, the evaluation may lead to changes such as the introduction of new rules or the elimination of certain rules. For example, an interpreter of the rules of etiquette may carve out new exceptions because it better serves the justifications laid out in the interpretive stage. An interpreter, then, may determine that putting one's elbows on the dinner table is acceptable and its prohibition was a mistake in the light of the justification of the rules of etiquette. Similarly, the interpreter could add rules or change them. *Id.* at 66.

Dworkin seeks at the interpretative stage a justification for institutions or practices, particularly the practice of law, which will show that institution or practice in its best light, or make the most of the institution or practice. The justification and interpretation must have what Dworkin describes as fit. *Id.* at 67. A person interpreting Shakespeare's play, Hamlet, for example, wants an understanding or theory of it which will make the most of it as a dramatic production. Nevertheless, the theory or understanding must interpret Hamlet and fit that play rather than transform it into "Midsummer's Night's Dream." Between several alternate interpretations of the same institution or practice all of which have some reasonable fit, one would choose, if one is interpreting law, on the basis of which one offers the higher moral justification and therefore makes the best of the institution of law. The justification need not fit every aspect of law; some legal decisions could be treated as mistakes. But the interpretation should offer a justification for most of the principal aspects of current law. The justification offered by the interpretation will support and offer an understanding of both the clear instances of legal concepts and the foundation for deciding hard cases. The difference between the core and penumbra, then, disappears under Dworkin's analysis in *Law's Empire.* Both our understanding of the core and penumbral area decisions concerning important legal concepts regarding human rights, for example, would be supported by the same justification arising from the same interpretation. The ultimate reason supporting rights or reasons, then, is the judge's interpretation of law, his general theory which has institutional fit but strives to make the most of the present materials of law as discerned at the preinterpretative stage as can be made of them. *Id.* at 65-68.

133. *Law's Empire, supra* note 16 at 114-17, 150. Conventionalism resembles H.L.A. Hart's understanding of law now treated by Dworkin as an interpretation of law at the interpretative stage rather than as a semantic theory concerning the words and materials as accepted by everyone at the preinterpretative stage. Like Hart's understanding that legal concepts and rules have a clear core meaning and a penumbral area where the judge using strong discretion may decide whether or not they apply, conventionalism perceives law as the product of past political decisions whose clear content at some point comes to an end leaving judges and other decision makers free to create new law. Where law is unclear or disputable there is no clear law binding on judges and they should not pretend that the new law they are making flows out of past statutes or cases. *Id.* at 118. By sternly recognizing the authority of clear past law and by not mudding it by trying unduly to extend it judges best preserve the authority of law and the rule of

law. *Id.* at 114-50.

Dworkin criticizes conventionalism as he describes it as lacking institutional fit; it does not describe our practices well. *Id.* at 120, 130-35. Judges regularly give more weight in justifying their decisions to past cases, statutes, and particularly constitutional provisions than conventionalism allows. Furthermore, conventionalism does not give weight to principles, reasons, supporting established rights and hence is unwilling to recognize the authority of those principles in disputable cases concerning rights. To this extent conventionalism does not take rights seriously. *Id.*

134. *Law's Empire, supra* note 16 at 151-55, 175. Dworkin offers a broad, perhaps too broad, definition of legal pragmatism as an interpretative theory. Dworkin describes pragmatism as taking a skeptical attitute towards past political decisions as a justification for judicial decision making. The Pragmatist, in Dworkin's view, regards action as the supreme good and consistency or knowledge as a mere instrument of a successul activity. The pragmatic approach justifies the state's coercive power by the decision itself and regards consistency, higher moral standards, and past political decisions as ancillary issues. *Id.* at 151. That definition would apparently apply to most Crits and to some natural lawyers as well as to some of those traditionally considered pragmatist. Some traditional pragmatists would give much more weight to authority than Dworkin's definition concedes. Some Crits share the pragmatist tradition; others would not. *See* Tushnet, "An Essay on Rights" 62 *Tex. L. Rev.* 1363 (1984); *see* also Horowitz, "The Bork Nomination and American Constitutional History" 39 *Syracuse L. Rev.* 1029 (1988). Pragmatism as Dworkin describes it is a law without rights and hence although it is appealing on the ground of justice or efficiency or wealth maximization it lacks institutional fit and ultimately does not make the most and best that can be made of our law and legal institutions. *Law's Empire, supra* note 16 at 160.

135. *Law's Empire, supra* note 16 at 176-224.

136. *Id.* at 254-258; *see Id.* at 225-275.

137. *Id.* at 230.

138. *Law's Empire, supra* note 16 at 225-275; *see Id.* at 397-399.

139. Compare *Id.* at 276-312 with *Id.* at 355-399; *see Id.* at 312, 397-399.

140. *Id.*

141. *See, Summers, supra* note 18.

142. *See Summers, supra* note 18 at 26-27. Summers confines his valuable study of the pragmatic-instrumentalists to the period before 1940. Arguably this prevented him from dealing with a number of developments in what could be described as creative legal realism which took place after that date. Realists who were concerned originally with predicting judicial behavior (the real rules as opposed to the paper rules) moved ultimately to studies of how judges ought to behave, for example, to a concern for the craftsmanship of appellate judges. The discovery that judges were human made in their effort to predict the behavior of judges carried over to their studies of judicial craftsmanship. There the concern with craftsmanship, with how things are done, became a concern with the human element in law, with what Jerome Frank has described as three dimensional law. The endeavor to understand the efforts of human judges seeking to understand human problems is a characteristic of legal realists that differentiates them from sociological jurisprudence. See Llewellyn, *Jurisprudence, supra* note 10 at 43,222; Donnelly, Book Review 3 Hofstra L. Rev. 899 (1975) (Reviewing W. Twining, *Karl Llewellyn and the Realist Movement* (1973) and D. Wigdor, *Roscoe Pound: Philosopher of Law.*(1973). [hereinafter Book Review]

143. *Summers, supra* note 18 at 69-80.

144. *See text infra* note 185-203.

145. *Taking Rights Seriously, supra* note 11 at 82-84.

146. *Taking Rights Seriously, supra* note 11 at 22-23, 82-84.

147. *Id.*

148. *Law's Empire, supra* note 16 at 95-96, 151-64.

149. *Declaration of Human Rights, supra* note 17.

150. *Id.* at preamble. One should recognize, of course, that the Universal Declaration of Human Rights is a resolution of the General Assembly and not a treaty imposing obligations on states. See A. H. Robertson, *Human Rights in the World* at 27 (1989). The Declaration was followed by the Covenant on Economic, Social and Cultural Rights and the Covenant on Civil and Political Rights which would when agreed to as treaties impose obligations on states. Nevertheless the use of goal language in describing both economic and social and political rights is worth noting.

151. *Declaration of Human Rights, supra* note 17 at Article 3.

152. *Id.* at Article 9. The Articles state the universal goals to be pursued, "....to secure their universal and effective recognition and

observance...." *Id.* at preamble.
153. *Id.* at Article 22.
154. Id. at Article 25(1).
155. *See* S. Hoffman, *Duties Beyond Borders* 100-05, 141-65 (1981).
156. J. Rawls, *A Theory of Justice* 60 (1971) [hereinafter cited as *Rawls*].
157. *Id.* at 60.
158. *Id.*
159. *Id.* at 61.
160. *A Theory of Justice, supra* note 156 at 61.
161. *Id.* at 244.
162. *See supra* note 142.
163. *Summers, supra* note 18 at 26-28, 137-159.
164. *Id.* at 161.
165. *Id.* at 244-50.
166. *Id.* at 63.
167. *Summers, supra* note 18 at 251. (Summers quotes Holmes "whatever the crowd wants"); see also W. James, "The Moral Philosopher and the Moral Life," in *The Writings of William James* 617, 623.
168. *Summers, supra* note 18 at 80.
169. *The Common Law Tradition, supra* note 50.
170. *Summers, supra* note 18 at 167. The author finds merit in this view; "hard cases" in penumbral areas can be decided by the judge's choice between competing social goals, based on his established consistent principles. See *Taking Rights Seriously, supra* note 11 at 81-130.
171. *U. S. Const.* amend. XIV, § 1.
172. *Plessy v. Ferguson*, 163 U.S. 537 (1896).
173. *See id.* at 551. The court, cited the Court of Appeals of New York in *People v. Gallagher*, 93 N.Y. 437, 448 (1883). "[w]hen the government, therefore, has secured to each of its citizens equal rights before the law and equal opportunities for improvement and progress, it has accomplished the end for which it was organized and performed all of the functions respecting social advantages with which it is endowed."
174. *Brown v. Board of Education*, 347 U.S. 483.
175. *Id.* at 483-95. The court states "[t]o separate them from others of similar age and qualifications solely because of their race generates a

feeling of inferiority as to their status in the community that may affect their hearts and minds in a way unlikely ever to be undone... We conclude that in the field of public education the doctrine of 'separate but equal' has no place. Separate educational facilities are inherently unequal." *Id.* at 494-95.

176. *New York Times v. Sullivan*, 376 U.S. 254 (1963).

177. *Id.* at 256.

178. *Id.* at 257-59.

179. *Id.* at 279-80.

180. *New York Times v. Sullivan*, 376 U.S. 254, 270.

181. *Brown v. Board of Education*, 347 U.S. 483.

182. *New York Times v. Sullivan*, 376 U.S. 254.

183. *Brown v. Board of Education*, 347 U.S. 483, 493.

184. *See Bickel, supra* note 78 at 22-35, 56-65.

185. *Taking Rights Seriously, supra* note 11 at 132.

186. *See The Concept of Law, supra* note 47 and accompanying text.

187. *Summers, supra* note 18 at 36-37.

188. *See* M. Twain, *The Adventures of Huckleberry Finn*, Cleveland Fine Editions Press, 377 (1947).

189. *Id.*

190. *Taking Rights Seriously, supra* note 11 at 85.

191. *Id.* at 85-86.

192. *Brown v. Board of Education*, 347 U.S. 483

193. *See Law's Empire, supra* note 16 at 381-397; *Cf. Taking Rights Seriously, supra* note 11 at 134-36.

194. *See Bickel supra* note 184; see also *Wechsler supra* note 78.

195. *Cf. Brown v. Board of Education*, 347 U.S. 483, 493-94.

196. *Summers, supra* note 18 at 170. If principles concern origins, the foundations of one's thinking and one's commitments, then Summers' suggestion provides a principled foundation for means-goal reasoning.

197. *Rawls, supra* note 160 at 250.

198. *Summers supra* note 18 at 170. Summers suggestion then, may reduce the ill effects of majoritarianism, and bring a consistency and cadence to the evolution of the law, minimizing overaction to ephemeral social needs.

199. *See Id.* Cf. Donnelly, Book Review: "The Inner Experience of Law, A Jurisprudence of Subjectivity, By David Granfield (1988)" 36 *Am.J. Jurisprudence* 239, 245 (1991).

200. *Rawls, supra* note 160 at 250.

201. *Id.* at 64-65.
202. Compare the discussion of interest group use of rights as resources *infra* notes 219-241 and accompanying text.
203. *See infra* text accompanying notes 427-429; 463-472.
204. Richard A. Posner, *The Problems of Jurisprudence* (1990) [hereinafter *The Problems of Jurisprudence*].
205. *Id.* at 454-69.
206. *Id.* at 462-63; See also R. Posner, "What Has Pragmatism to Offer Law?" *Pragmatism in Law and Society* (edited by M. Brint and W. Weaver) Westview Press 1991. In tracing the historical origins of pragmatism, Judge Posner begins with Charles Sanders Pierce and Nicholas St. John Green. He notes that prior to these thinkers, anticipation of pragmatism can be found in Epicurus and other philosophers of that age. An elucidation of pragmatism was then offered by William James, John Dewey, George Mead, and F.S.C. Schiller. John Dewey, in the tradition of New England liberalism, joined pragmatism and legal realism in his essay on law. The lasting influence of the New England pragmatists, James and Dewey, led to the development of legal realism. Oliver W. Holmes Jr., James and Pierce were members of the Cambridge Metaphysical Club and were an inspiration to the legal realists. The legal realist movement was joined by John Chipman Grey, Cardozo, Jerome Frank, William Douglas, Karl Llewellyn, Felix Cohen and Max Radin. However, as Posner points out, by the end of World War II pragmatism and legal realism were to a great extent abandoned. The dominant schools of thought became logical positivism and other analytic philosophy. The move away from pragmatism ended by the 1960s. At this point pragmatism found a great proponent in Richard Rorty, followed in the 1970s by the critical legal studies movement. The Crits, led by Duncan Kennedy, were the radical offspring of legal realism. The 1980s developed a new breed of pragmatists that included Martha Minnow, Thomas Grey, Daniel Farber, Philip Frickey, and others. Posner includes himself as a neopragmatist and notes that Professor Rorty has even included Ronald Dworkin in this group. It is important to note, however, that Dworkin does not consider himself a member of this intellectually diverse group and even labels this philosophic tradition as intellectually bankrupt.
207. *See supra* notes 141-148 and accompanying text.
208. *See supra* notes 128-140 and accompanying text.

209. *See The Problems of Jurisprudence, supra* note 204 at 105-108.
210. *Id.* at 197-203; *Cf. Law's Empire, supra* note 16 at 154-155 et. sec.
211. *Id.* at 137-39.
212. *See* Definition and Theory, *supra* note 9 at 41-45.
213. *See The Common Law Tradition, supra* note 50 at 214; *see also Jurisprudence supra* note 10 at 233 note b., 318-22, 323-51.
214. O. W. Holmes, The Path of the Law, 10 *Harv. L. Rev.* 457, 459, (1897).
215. *See infra* text accompanying notes 317-327.
216. *See* Definition and Theory, *supra* note 9 at 41-45.
217. *See Rawls supra* note 156.
218. *See Taking Rights Seriously, supra* note 11 at 87.
219. *See Scheingold, supra* note 24.
220. *Scheingold, supra* note 24 at 6.
221. *Id* at 204.
222. *Id.*
223. *Id.*
224. *Scheingold, supra* note 24 at 204.
225. *Id.*
226. *Id.*
227. *Id.* at 205.
228. *Scheingold, supra* note 24 at 13-79.
229. *Id.*
230. *Id.* at 84.
231. *Id.* at 90.
232. *Scheingold, supra* note 24 at 90-91.
233. *See Id.* at 184-85.
234. *Brown v. Board of Education*, 347 U.S. 483.
235. *Cf. Scheingold, supra* note 24 at 143-48, (discussing the organization of the civil rights movement and the *Brown* decision).
236. *See Id.* at 170-73.
237. *See Id.* at 4-5.
238. *See Id.* at 13-79 (discussing the Myth of Rights).
239. *Cf. Scheingold supra* note 24 at 14-15. The myth of rights "has the power to confer legitimacy,....". *Id.* at 14.
240. *See Id.* at 173-74, (discussing the American Civil Liberties Union (ACLU) and the National Association for the Advancement of Colored People (NAACP).

241. *See, e.g.*, *Id.* at 105-6, (discussing law and lawyering as assisting the activation of the poor in asserting claims of rights).
242. Horwitz, "The Bork Nomination and American Constitutional History," 39 *Syracuse L. Rev.* 1029, 1036-37 (1988), [hereinafter Horwitz].
243. *Id.*
244. O. W. Holmes, Jr., *The Common Law* 1 (1881) [hereinafter *The Common Law*].
245. Horwitz, *supra* note 242 at 1037.
246. *Id.* at 1038.
247. *Id.* at 1034.
248. *Id.* at 1037.
249. Horwitz, *supra* note 242 at 1037.
250. *Id.* at 1039.
251. *Id.* at 1039.
252. Tushnet, "An Essay on Rights," 62 *Tex. L. Rev.* 1363 (1984) [hereinafter Tushnet].
253. *Id.* at 1364.
254. *Id.* at 1364-71.
255. *Id.* at 1370.
256. Tushnet, *supra* note 252 at 1379.
257. *Id.* at 1393.
258. *Id.* at 1392.
259. *Id.*
260. Unger, "The Critical Legal Studies Movement," 96 *Harv. L. Rev.* 563 (1983) [hereinafter Unger].
261. *Id.* at 597.
262. *See supra* notes 260-262 and accompanying text.
263. *See supra* text accompanying notes 242-261.
264. Compare *supra* text accompanying notes 76-139.
265. *Id.*
266. *See* Donnelly, *supra* note 1.
267. *See Taking Rights Seriously supra* note 11, Chap. 5., Constitutional Cases, at 131 to 149.
268. *See supra* notes 245-249.
269. *See supra* text accompanying notes 219-241.
270. *See supra* note 4; See C.A. MacKinnon, "Feminism, Marxism, Method, and the State; An Agenda for Theory," 7 *Signs: Journal of Women, Culture and Society* 515-544 (1982); Margaret J. Radin, "The

Pragmatist and the Feminist," in *Pragmatism in Law and Society* 127-153 (Michael Brint and William Weaver, eds., 1991).

271. *See supra* note 5; one current form of Outsider Jurisprudence would be Critical Race Theory.

272. *See* L. Bender, From Gender Difference to Feminist Solidarity: Using Carol Gilligan and an Ethic of Care in Law, 15 *Vermont L. Rev.* 1-48 (1990).

273. *See infra*, text accompanying notes 284-286.

274. *See Heracles' Bow*, *supra* note 6 at ix-xvi.

275. *Id.* at *xii.*

276. *Id.* at 3-27.

277. *Id.* at 5.

278. *Id.* at 215-237.

279. *Id.* at 225.

280. *See Taking Rights Seriously, supra* note 11 at 180.

281. *See Heracles' Bow, supra* note 6 at xii

282. *See supra* text, accompanying notes 219-241.

283. *See supra*, text accompanying notes 242-269.

284. *See supra* note 270.

285. *See supra* note 271.

286. *See supra* note 34.

III. Horizons-New Model

287. *See infra* note 289-296 and accompanying text.

288. *See infra* note 317-327 and accompanying text.

289. *See* Donnelly, *supra* note 1 at 254-263; *see also* B. Lonergan, *Method in Theology* 235-37 (1972); *see also* D. Tracy, *The Achievement of Bernard Lonergan* 1-21, 104-32 (1970); *see also* M. Heidegger, *Identity and Difference* 34-5 (1969).

290. *See Donnelly, supra* note 1 at 257.

291. B. Lonergan, *Method in Theology*, 235-37 (1972) (hereinafter Methods).

292. *Id.*

293. Horizons are dependent on a three-fold division which appears at any state of the knowledge process: First, the known, i.e., the range of questions I can raise and answer. Second, the known unknown, i.e., the range of questions I can raise, find significant, find possible ways of solving but, in fact, cannot as yet answer. In more traditional vocabulary this is the area of doctra ignorantia. Third, the unknown unknown, i.e., the range of questions that I do not and, in fact, cannot

raise as they lack significance for me--are literally meaningless to me. Traditionally stated, this is the area of indocta ignorantia. As a first approximation, therefore, horizons may be called the limit or boundary between my docta and indocta ignorantia. As a second approximation, it is to be noted that what lies beyond my horizon consists not principally of answers but of questions that are meaningless and insignificant to me. Tracy, *The Achievement of Bernard Lonergan*, 9-10 (1970) [hereinafter Tracy].

294. Donnelly, *supra* note 1 at 255.

295. *Id.* at 256.

296. *Methods, supra* note 291 at 254, n.250.

297. Donnelly, *supra* note 1 at 257.

298. *Brown v. Board of Education* 347 U.S. 483 (1954).

299. *Terry v. Ohio,* 392 U.S. 1 (1968).

300. See Donnelly, *supra* note 1 at 259-60.

301. *Id.* at 259.

302. See Donnelly, *supra* note 1 at 260-61.

303. *See Tracy, supra* note 293 at 104-32; *see also* B. Lonergan, *Insight* 13-19, 233-34, 257, 374, 439 (3d ed. 1970) [hereinafter *Insights*].

304. "Thus, those whose horizons are foreign to Heracles will have difficulty presenting their needs and concerns to him precisely because of his consistent theory. Instead, an appeal to him can best be made in terms of his theory and the principles it recognizes." Donnelly, *supra* note 1 at 259; *see Taking Rights Seriously, supra* note 11 at 125-30.

305. Crossing horizons is a result of becoming familiar and moving into the viewpoint of a new and unfamiliar horizon.

306. *See Taking Rights Seriously, supra* note 11 at 115-23, see also Donnelly *supra* note 1 at 259.

307. Donnelly, *supra* note 1 at 259-60.

308. *Id.* at 260-61.

309. *Id.*

310. *See* C. Fifoot, *Lord Mansfield* (1936).

311. Book Review, *supra* note 142 at 910.

312. *Id.*

313. *See supra* note 302 and accompanying text.

314. *See supra* note 264-276 and accompanying text.

315. *Id.*

316. *See* Critical Legal Studies Movement, *supra* note 31.

317. *See* Definition and Theory, *supra* note 9 at 41-49.
318. *See Id.*
319. *Id.* at 42, *see supra* note 22 and accompanying text.
320. *Id.*
321. *See e.g., Scheingold, supra* note 24.
322. *See Concept of Law, supra* note 47 at 1-5.
323. *See Scheingold, supra* note 24 at 3.
324. *See Concept of Law, supra* note 47 at 1-17.
325. *See Jurisprudence, supra* note 10.
326. *See The Common Law Tradition, supra* note 50.
327. *See Taking Rights Seriously, supra* note 11.
328. *See The Common Law Tradition, supra* note 50 at 77-91.
329. *See* Kennedy, *supra* note 29.
330. *See e.g.*, Donnelly & Donnelly, *1987 Survey of New York Law, Commercial Law* 39 *Syracuse L. Rev.* 161-71 (1988); Donnelly & Donnelly, *1988 Survey of New York Law, Commercial Law,* 40 *Syracuse L. Rev.* 143-51 (1989); Donnelly & Donnelly, *1990 Survey of New York Law, Commercial Law* 42 *Syracuse L. Rev.* 411-19 (1991).
331. *See e.g.*, Donnelly & Donnelly, *1983 Survey of New York Law, Commercial Law* 25 *Syracuse L. Rev.* 161-65 (1984); Donnelly & Donnelly, *1985 Survey of New York Law, Commercial Law* 37 *Syracuse L. Rev.* 356-59 (1986); Donnelly & Donnelly, *1987 Survey of New York Law, Commercial Law,* 39 *Syracuse L. Rev.* 209-17 (1988); Donnelly & Donnelly, *1990 Survey of New York Law, Commercial Law* 42 *Syracuse L. Rev.* 447-53 (1991).
332. *See e.g.*, Donnelly & Donnelly, *1984 Survey of New York Law, Commercial Law* 36 *Syracuse L. Rev.* 82-85 (1985).
333. *Supra* note 9-24 and accompanying text.
334. *See Heracles' Bow, supra* note 6 at xii, xiii.
335. *Concept of Law supra* note 47.
336. *Id.* at 121-32.
337. *See e.g.*, Fuller, "Positivism and Fidelity to Law--A Reply to Professor Hart" 71 *Harv. L. Rev.* 630, 661-69 (1958) [hereinafter *Positivism and Fidelity to Law*].
338. *Id.*
339. *See supra* note 25-32, 242-278 and accompanying text.
340. *See supra* notes 128-132 and accompanying text.
341. *See supra* notes 132-135 and accompanying text.
342. *See* Hart, Positivism and the Separation of Law and Morals" 71

Harv. L. Rev. 593, 607-611 (1958); *See also Concept of Law, supra* note 47 at 125-26.
343. *See* Fuller Positivism and Fidelity to Law, *supra* note 337 at 662-64.
344. Hart, "Positivism and the Separation of Law and Morals" 71 *Harv. L. Rev.* 593, 607 (1958) [hereinafter *Separation of Law and Morals*].
345. *Id.*
346. *Positivism and Fidelity to Law, supra* note 337 at 663.
347. *Id.* at 663-64.
348. *See Law's Empire, supra* note 16 at 114-175.
349. *See supra* text accompanying notes 8-34.
350. *See Law's Empire, supra* note 16 at 176-275.
351. *Id.* at 65-68.
352. *Id.* at 195-202.
353. Kennedy *supra* note 29 at 518-19.
354. *See Heracles' Bow, supra* note 6.
355. *The Common Law Tradition, supra* note 50.
356. *See Concept of Law, supra* note 47.
357. *See The Common Law Tradition, supra* note 50; *see also Jurisprudence, supra* note 10.
358. *See Scheingold, supra* note 24.
359. *See Taking Rights Seriously, supra* note 11; *see also Law's Empire, supra* note 16.
360. *See supra* notes 242-278 and accompanying text.
361. *See Heracles' Bow, supra* note 6.
362. *See The Concept of Law, supra* note 47.
363. *Id.*
364. *See* Definition and Theory, *supra* note 9.
365. *See Jurisprudence, supra* note 10 at 39-41.
366. *See The Common Law Tradition, supra* note 50 at 17-18.
367. *See* Book Review, *supra* note 142 at 909-11.
368. *See e.g., The Impact of Supreme Court Decisions* (T. Becker & M. Treely 2d ed. 1973).
369. *See Book Review, supra* note 142 at 915-16.
370. *Id.* at 914-15.
371. *See Scheingold, supra* note 24.
372. *Taking Rights Seriously, supra* note 11.
373. *The Concept of Law, supra* note 47.

374. *Taking Rights Seriously, supra* note 11 at 81-130.
375. *See* Donnelly, *supra* note 1 at 221-22.
376. *See Taking Rights Seriously, supra* note 11 at 81-205.
377. *See* Separation of Law and Morals, *supra* note 2. (Wherein Hart takes a utilitarian position.)
378. *The Concept of Law, supra* note 47 at 121-150.
379. *See Id.* at 131-32; Separation of Law and Morals, *supra* note 2 at 612, 626-29; *c.f. Taking Rights Seriously, supra* note 11 at 82.
380. *Law's Empire, supra* note 16 at 37-46, see Id. 114-150.
381. *Id.* at 34-35, 45-46.
382. *Id.* at 114-150.
383. *Id.* at 176-275.
384. *Supra* notes 141-148 and accompanying text.
385. O. W. Holmes, "The Path of the Law," 10 *Harv. L. Rev.* 457 (1897).
386. *Id.* at 461.
387. *Id.* at 467.
388. *Id.*
389. *Summers, supra* note 18 at 62-66.
390. *See* Book Review, *supra* note 142 at 916.
391. *See Summers, supra* note 18 at 31.
392. *See* Book Review, *supra* note 142 at 900.
393. *Summers, supra* note 18 at 31.
394. *See* Book Review, *supra* note 142 at 906.
395. *See Id.*
396. J. Frank, *Courts on Trial* 74, 174-76, 182-83, 197-98 (1950) [hereinafter *Courts on Trial*].
397. *See Id.* at 176.
398. *See* Book Review, *supra* note 142 at 909-911, and accompanying notes; *See also, The Common Law Tradition,* Llewellyn comments "Hutchenson on 'the little small dice' can be read only by a moron as suggesting gambling probabilities. His insistence is on the frequent determinative character of factors not yet reduced to formula or to any other diagnosis which is communicable by more than such terms as 'hunch' or 'insight' or 'something'--all used in terms of responsible conscience and tradition. *The Common Law Tradition, supra* note 50 at 121 n.154; see also Hutcheson, "The Judgment Intuitive: The Function of the 'Hunch' in Judicial Decision," 14 *Cornell L.Q.* 274 (1929).

399. *See Jurisprudence, supra* note 10 at 222; *see also, The Common Law Tradition, supra* note 50 at 268-74; *see also*, Book Review, *supra* note 142 at 905-11.
400. *Id.*
401. *See* Donnelly, *supra* note 1 at 226.
402. *See Courts on Trial, supra* note 396 at 74, 182, 198; *See also, Donnelly, supra* note 1 at 229-31.
403. *See* Donnelly, *supra* note 1 at 236-37.
404. *See, Taking Rights Seriously, supra* note 11 at 125-26.
405. *See Summers, supra* note 18 at 185-87.
406. *See* Donnelly, *supra* note 1 at 292.
407. *See Law's Empire, supra* note 16 at 101, 151-175.
408. *See The Problems of Jurisprudence, supra* note 204 at 454-69; See also R. Posner, "What Has Pragmatism to Offer Law" and R. Dworkin, "Pragmatism, Right Answers, and True Banality" in Pragmatism in Law and Society 14-46 and 359-388 (Michael Brint and William Weaver eds. 1991).
409. *See Law's Empire, supra* note 16 at 255-57.
410. *See supra* note 408.
411. *See Law's Empire, supra* note 16 at 379-91.
412. *See The Problems of Jurisprudence, supra,* note 204 at 454-69.
413. *Supra* note 355-412 and accompanying text.
414. *Supra* note 9-34 and accompanying text.

IV. A Higher Interpretation

415. *Infra* note 418-442 and accompanying text.
416. *Infra* notes 443-451 and accompanying text.
417. *Infra* notes 451-489 and accompanying text.
418. *See e.g.*, Hart "Positivism and the Separation of Law and Morals," 71 *Harv. L. Rev.* 593 (1958); Fuller, "Positivism and Fidelity to Law--A Reply to Professor Hart" 71 *Harv. L. Rev.* 630 (1958); A. Hagerstrom, *Inquiries into The Nature of Law and Morals* (Broad Trans. 1953); Hart "Book Review" 30 *Philosophy* 369 (1955) (reviewing Hagerstrom, *Inquiries into The Nature of Law and Morals* (1953)); K. Olivecrona, *Law as Fact* (1939); Hart, "Scandinavian Realism" 1959 Cambridge L. J. 233 (1959).
419. *See The Concept of Law, supra* note 47 at 120-32.
420. *See The Common Law Tradition, supra* note 50 at 219-22.
421. *See The Concept of Law, supra* note 47 at 97-107.
422. Hans Kelsen, *Pure Theory of Law* 8-10, 193-95 (translated by

Max Knight, 2d ed. 1967).
423. *See Taking Rights Seriously, supra* note 11 at 116-117; *See Law's Empire, supra* note 16 at 225-27, 379-81.
424. *See Taking Rights Seriously, supra* note 11 at 106-107.
425. *See Id.;* Compare 132-37 with 81-130; *See* Donnelly, *supra* note 1 at 245-47.
426. *See Law's Empire, supra* note 16 at 254-58; *see Id.* 228-32.
427. *See* Donnelly, *supra* note 2 at 285-86.
428. *See Summers, supra* note 18 at 41-59.
429. *See* Donnelly, *supra* note 1 at 225-253.
430. *See* Book Review, *supra* note 142 at 906-11.
431. *See Taking Rights Seriously, supra* note 11; *See Law's Empire, supra* note 16.
432. Kennedy, *supra* note 29.
433. Id. at 518-27.
434. *See* Kennedy, *supra* note 29 at 522-527.
435. *See The Problems of Jurisprudence, supra* note 204.
436. *Id.* at 132, 356-92.
437. *See supra* note 7.
438. *See The Problems of Jurisprudence, supra* note 204 at 37-70.
439. *See Id.* at 54, 61, 63, 107, 155-56, 167-70, 175, 257-59, 327-28, 353-91, 427, 434-35, 439-442.
440. *See Heracles' Bow, supra* note 6.
441. *See Id.* at 28-48.
442. *See supra* note 34.
443. *See Taking Rights' Seriously, supra* note 11 at 180, 150-83; *See Law's Empire, supra* note 16 at 195-215.
444. *See Law's Empire, supra* note 16 at 195-202.
445. *See L. Fuller Anatomy of Law*, 73-76 (1968); *see also* Donnelly, supra note 1 at 240-42..
446. 347 U.S. 483 (1954).
447. *See Scheingold, supra* note 24 at 3-33.
448. *See Id.* at 83-143.
449. *See supra* notes 171-184 and accompanying text.
450. *See* L. Fuller, *Anatomy of Law,* 73-76 (1968)*; see also* Donnelly, *supra* note 1 at 240-42.
451. *See The Concept of Law, supra* note 47 at 86-88.
452. *Id.* at 22-23, 80-81.
453. *See Id.* at 87-88.

454. *Id.* at 87.
455. *See* W. Hohfeld, *Fundamental Legal Conceptions* (1919).
456. *Id.* at 36.
457. *Id.* at 38.
458. *See Id.* at vii-xv, (Arthur L. Corbin's Foreward, discussing Hohfeld's influence and contribution).
459. *See Hohfeld, supra* note 455 at 31.
460. Bear in mind that X's claim of a right may be viewed from any number of perspectives, and that under another appropriate normal theory X may have a right.
461. *See Jurisprudence, supra* 10 at 3-74.
462. *See* Definition and Theory, *supra* note 9 at 42-43.
463. *See Law's Empire, supra* note 16 at 151-175.
464. *See supra* note 134-140 and accompanying text.
465. *See supra* note 162-184 and accompanying text.
466. *Taking Rights Seriously, supra* note 11 at 22-23, 82-84.
467. *See Id.* at 84.
468. *See supra* notes 155-161, 200-202 and accompanying text.
469. *See supra* notes 141-144 and accompanying text.
470. *See supra* notes 196-199 and accompanying text.
471. *See supra* notes 204-211 and accompanying text.
472. *See supra* notes 242-278 and accompanying text.
473. *See* preceding paragraph discussion of Posner and rights..
474. *See supra* notes 10, 48-55 and accompanying text.
475. Kennedy, *supra* note 29.
476. *See supra* notes 9-34 and accompanying text.
477. *Cf.* note 9 and accompanying text.
478. *Cf.* note 10 and accompanying text.
479. *Cf.* note 11 and accompanying text.
480. *Cf.* notes 12-16 and accompanying text.
481. *Cf.* notes 17-21 and accompanying text.
482. *Cf.* note 24 and accompanying text.
483. *See supra* notes 219-230 and accompanying text.
484. *Cf.* notes 22-23 and accompanying text.
485. *Cf.* notes 33-34 and accompanying text.
486. *See* Definition and Theory, *supra* note 9 at 43.
487. *See Taking Rights Seriously, supra* note 11 at 84-88, 131-49.
488. *See Law's Empire, supra* note 16 at 225-75.
489. *See Heracles' Bow, supra* note 4 at xii, 28, 32-35, 37.

Overview and Conclusion

490. *See supra* notes 1-286 and accompanying text.
491. *See supra* notes 1-286 and accompanying text.
492. *See supra* notes 287-414 and accompanying text.
493. *See supra* notes 451-489 and accompanying text.
494. *See supra* notes 287-414 and accompanying text.

Bibliography

BOOKS

Becker, T. & Treely, M. (eds.), *The Impact of Supreme Court Decisions*, 2d ed., 1973.

Bickel, A., *The Least Dangerous Branch: The Supreme Court at the Bar of Politics*, 2d ed., Yale University Press, New Haven, 1986.

Brint, M. & Weaver, W. (eds.), *Pragmatism in Law and Society*, Westview Press, 1991.

Dworkin, R., *Laws Empire*, Harvard University Press, Cambridge, 1986.
_____. *Taking Rights Seriously*, Harvard University Press, Cambridge, 1977.

Fifoot, C., *Lord Mansfield*, The Clarendon Press, Oxford, 1936.

Frank, J., *Courts on Trial: Myth and Reality in American Justice*, Princeton University Press, Princeton, 1950.

Fuller, L., *Anatomy of Law*, F.A. Praeger, Princeton, 1968.

______. *The Morality of Law*, Yale University Press, New Haven, 1964.

Hagerstrom, A., *Inquiries into The Nature of Law and Morals*, (trans. Broad), London, 1953.

Hart, H. L. A., *The Concept of Law*, Clarendon Press, Oxford, 1961.

Heidegger, M., *Identity and Difference*, Harper and Row, New York, 1969.

Hoffman, S., *Duties Beyond Borders*, Syracuse University Press, Syracuse, 1981.

Hohfeld, W., *Fundamental Legal Conceptions*, Yale University Press, New Haven, 1919.

Holmes, O.W. Jr., *The Common Law*, Little, Brown, Boston, 1881.

Kelsen, H., *Pure Theory of Law*, (trans. Max Knight), 2d ed., University of California Press, Berkeley, 1967.

Llewellyn, K., *Jurisprudence Realism in Theory and Practice*, University of Chicago Press, Chicago, 1962.
______. *The Common Law Tradition: Deciding Appeals*, Little, Brown, Boston, 1960.

Lonergan, B., *Method in Theology*, Dayton, Longman, & Todd, London, 1972.
______. *Insight*, 3d ed., Harper and Row, New York, 1970.

Minow, M., *Making All the Difference: Inclusion, Exclusion and American Law*, Cornell University Press, Ithaca, 1990.

Olivecrona, K., *Law as Fact*, Stevens, London, 1971.

Posner, R., *The Economics of Justice*, Harvard University Press, Cambridge, 1981.

_______. *Law and Literature: A Misunderstood Relation*, Harvard University Press, Cambridge, 1988.

_______. *The Problems of Jurisprudence*, Harvard University Press, Cambridge, 1990.

_______. *Sex and Reason*, Harvard University Press, Cambridge, 1992.

Rawls, J., *A Theory of Justice*, Belknap Press of Harvard University Press, Cambridge, 1971.

Robertson, A.H., *Human Rights in the World*, 3d ed., Manchester University Press, Manchester, 1989.

Scheingold, S., *The Politics of Rights*, Yale University Press, New Haven, 1974.

Summers, R., *Instrumentalism and American Legal Theory*, Cornell University Press, Ithaca, 1982.

Tracy, D., *The Achievement of Bernard Lonergan*, Herder & Herder, New York, 1970.

Twain, M., *The Adventures of Huckleberry Finn*, Fine Editions Press, Cleveland, 1947.

Twining, W., *Karl Llewellyn and the Realist Movement*,

Weidenfeld and Nicolson, London, 1973.

White, J.B., *Heracles' Bow Essays on the Rhetoric and Poetics of the Law*, 1985.

Wiecek, W., *Constitutional Development in a Modernizing Society: The United States,1803 to 1917*, American Historical Association, Washington, D.C., 1985.
______. *A Great and Stately Jurisdiction*, (unpublished manuscript).

Wigdor, D., *Roscoe Pound: Philosopher of Law*, Greenwood Press, Westport, 1973.

Articles

Bender, L., "From Gender Difference to Feminist Solidarity: Using Carol Gilligan and an Ethic of Care in Law, 15 *Vermont L. Rev.* 1 (1990).

Donnelly, S., "Book Review, *36 Am. J. Jurisprudence* 239 (1991) (reviewing D. Granfield, *The Inner Experience of Law, A Jurisprudence of Subjectivity* (1988))
____, "Principles, Persons, and Horizons: A Friendly Analysis of What Dworkin Has Overlooked, 26 *St. Louis U. L. J.* 217 (1982).
____, "A Theory of Justice, Judicial Methodology, and the Constitutionality of Capital Punishment: Rawls, Dworkin, and a Theory of Criminal Responsibility, 29 *Syracuse. L. Rev.* 1109 (1978).
____,"Book Review, 3 *Hofstra L. Rev.* 899 (1975) (reviewing W. Twining, *Karl Llewellyn and the Realist Movement* (1973)).

Donnelly, S. and M.A. Donnelly, "1990 Survey of New York Law, Commercial Law, 42 *Syracuse L. Rev.* 411 (1991). "1988 Survey of New York Law, Commercial Law, 40 *Syracuse L. Rev.* 143 (1989). "1987 Survey of New York Law, Commercial Law, 39 *Syracuse L. Rev.* 161 (1988) "1985 Survey of New York Law, Commercial Law, 37 *Syracuse L. Rev.* 356 (1986). "1984 Survey of New York Law, Commercial Law, 36 *Syracuse L. Rev.* 82 (1985). "1983 Survey of New York Law, Commercial Law, 25 *Syracuse L. Rev.* 161 (1984).

Dworkin, R., "Pragmatism, Right Answers, and True Banality, *Pragmatism in Law and Society* (edited by M. Brint and W. Weaver) Westview Press 1991.

____, "No Right Answer, 53 *N.Y.U. L. Rev.* 1 (1978).

____, "Seven Critics, 11 *Ga. L. Rev.* 1201 (1977).

____, "Hard Cases, 88 *Harv. L. Rev.* 1057 (1975).

Fuller, L., "Positivism and Fidelity to Law- A Reply to Professor Hart, 71 *Harv. L. Rev.* 630 (1958).

Hart, H.L.A., "American Jurisprudence Through English Eyes: The Nightmare and the Noble Dream, 11 *Ga. L. Rev.* 969 (1977).

____, "Scandinavian Realism, 1959 *Cambridge L. J.* 233 (1959).

____, "Positivism and the Separation of Law and Morals, 71 *Harv. L. Rev.* 593 (1958).

____, "Definition and Theory in Jurisprudence, 70 *Law. Q. Rev.* 37 (1954).

____, "Book Review, 30 *Philosophy* 369 (1955) (reviewing A. Hagerstrom, *Inquiries into The Nature of Law and Morals* (1953)).

Holmes, O.W. Jr., "The Path of the Law, 10 *Harv. L. Rev.* 457 (1897).

Horwitz, M., "The Bork Nomination and American Constitutional History, 39 *Syracuse L. Rev.* 1027 (1988).

Hutcheson, "The Judgment Intuitive: The Function of the `Hunch' in Judicial Decision, 14 *Cornell L. Q.* 274 (1929).

Kennedy, D., "Freedom and Constraint in Adjudication: A Critical Phenomenology, 36 *J. Legal Educ.* 518 (1986).

Llewellyn, K., "Some Realism about Realism-Responding to Dean Pound, 44 *Harv. L. Rev.* 1222 (1931).
____, "A Realist Jurisprudence-The Next Step, 30 *Colum. L. Rev.* 431 (1930).

MacKinnon, C., "Feminism, Marxism, Method, and the State: An Agenda for Theory, 7 *Signs: Journal of Women, Culture and Society* 515 (1982).

Mastuda, M., "Public Response to Racist Speech: Considering the Victim's Story, 87 *Mich. L. Rev.* 2320 (1989).

Note, "Racist Speech, The first Amendment, and Public Universities: Taking a Stand on Neutrality, 76 *Cornell L. Rev.* 549 (1991).

Note, "'Round and 'Round the Bramble Bush: From Legal Realism to Critical Legal Scholarship, 96 *Harv. L.*

Rev. 1669 (1982).

Posner, R., "What Has Pragmatism to Offer Law? *Pragmatism in Law and Society* (edited by M. Brint and W. Weaver) Westview Press 1991.

____, "The Ethical Significance of Free Choice: A Reply to Professor West, 99 *Harv. L. Rev.* 1431 (1986).

____, "The Ethical and Political Basis of the Efficiency Norm in Common Law Adjudication, 8 *Hofstra L. Rev.* 487 (1980).

Radin, M., "The Pragmatist and the Feminist, *Pragmatism in Law and Society* (edited by M. Brint and W. Weaver) Westview Press 1991.

Tushnet, M., "An Essay on Rights, 62 *Texas L. Rev.* 1363 (1984).

____, "Following the Rules Laid Down: A Critique of Interpretivism and Neutral Principles, 96 *Harv. L. Rev.* 781 (1983).

Unger, R., "Critical Legal Studies Symposium, 36 *Stan. L. Rev.* 1 (1984).

____, "The Critical Legal Studies Movement, 96 *Harv. L. Rev.* 563 (1983).

Wechsler, H., "Toward Neutral Principles of Constitutional Law, 73 *Harv. L. Rev.* 1 (1959).

West, "The Supreme Court, 1989 Term, Taking Freedom Seriously, 104 *Harv. L. Rev.* 43 (1990).

____, "Law, Literature, and the Celebration of Authority (Bork Review Exchange) 83 *NW U. L. Rev.* 977 (1989).

____, "Jurisprudence and Gender, 55 *U. Chi. L. Rev.* 1 (1988).

____, "The Differences in Women's Hedonic Lives: A Phenomenological Critique of Feminist Legal Theory, 3 *Wis. Women's L. J.* 80 (1987).

____,"Submission, Choice, and Ethics: A Rejoinder to Judge Posner, 99 *Harv. L. Rev.* 1449 (1986).

____, "Authority, Autonomy, And Choice: The Role of Consent in the Moral and Political Visions of Franz Kafka and Richard Posner, 99 *Harv. L. Rev.* 384 (1985).

INDEX

About the Author

Samuel J. M. Donnelly is a Professor of Law at Syracuse University College of Law, a member of the New York and New Jersey bars with an LL.B. from Harvard Law School and an LL.M. from New York University School of Law. At the College of Law where he has taught since 1964, he teaches Jurisprudence and Commercial Law.